D0837452

The
Compulsive
Woman

Sandra Simpson LeSourd is a lecturer on chemical dependency and compulsive behavior. Formerly a Walt Disney artist and Miss Vermont, she is also the author of *The Not-So-Compulsive Woman*.

The Compulsive Woman

Sandra Simpson LeSourd

To
Brad
Brent
Lisa

© 1987, 1990 by Sandra Simpson LeSourd

Published by Fleming H. Revell
a division of Baker Book House Company
P.O. Box 6287, Grand Rapids, MI 49516-6287

Spire edition published 1996

Printed in the United States of America

ISBN 0-8007-8639-4

Contents

Introduction

Who is the compulsive woman?

The woman who volunteers for everything, who can't say no.

The woman whose TV is on all day long or who lives her life around soap operas.

The woman whose life revolves around food. She eats too much—or too little. Sweets are often her downfall.

The compulsive woman is an exercise nut, jogging miles every day, rain or shine. She is the one who shops when she needs a high while debts pile up. She may be a chain-smoker or a closet alcoholic, hooked on prescription drugs or sex or dependent on male approval for her sense of worth.

The compulsive woman is easy prey for psychics, spiritists, cults of every kind. She's a perfectionist who never lives up to her own expectations. Her natural drive and energy have become distorted; her motor is running wild. She has an irrational need to do something over and over to the point where she has lost control.

In other words, the compulsive woman has a complicated problem, and the solution to her problem has to address more than her primary addiction or symptom. According to a study done by *Ms.* magazine published in February 1987, "The patterns of dependence [for women] have been obscured by the tendency to look at individual addictions rather than the forces that create dependency. . . ."

One of the significant features of the *Ms.* survey was a precedent-setting demonstration that the compulsive personality expresses itself in more than one addiction. "Cross-addictions," that is, multiple or reinforcing addictions, are a tremendous problem for the compulsive woman; a cure is difficult so long as one tries to treat only the symptoms without getting at the root causes: fear, anger, and, in particular, shame.

Another significant feature in compulsion revealed in the *Ms.* study is the gender factor. The survey revealed that women are more likely to have certain kinds of addictions than men (shopping, watching television, compulsive eating and dieting, taking tranquilizers, etc.). More importantly, it revealed that there is a particular pattern in compulsion that most compulsive women demonstrate. "We are trained from early childhood to form at least part of our identity in terms of dependency," observes *Ms.*, "generally upon fathers, boyfriends, male bosses, or husbands who are older. . . ."

The compulsive woman is often addicted to love. Wrong love. Or she is dependent on men as the primary token of her value. And this pattern of dependency leads to lack of self-direction, self-control, and self-esteem.

I was led to a study of compulsive behavior not out of any abstract interest but through the desperate need to understand my own life and behavior. I had not one but all of the compulsions mentioned above. I was cross-addicted to almost *everything* at one time or another. The despair it caused led me at one point to try to kill myself. If some women can identify with my symptoms and my misery, I hope that my pathway to recovery will also inspire and encourage these women in their battle to gain mastery of themselves and their lives gone out of control.

It is possible for the compulsive woman to break the patterns that control her, to recover self-worth, and to lead a constructive and joyous life. That is the promise of this book.

Sandra Simpson LeSourd

Facing Off

*Many people operate in their daily lives as automatons,
almost completely unaware that their nearly every action is
dictated by compulsion, with little or no freedom of choice
and with virtually no spontaneity. Many people don't know
the difference between compulsion and choice. . . . {They}
are so overwhelmed and tyrannized by their compulsions
that they must act out (do things) immediately, impulsively,
without thought or consideration in order to overcome
complete and utter paralysis.*

Theodore Isaac Rubin, M.D.
The Winner's Notebook

AS I WALKED UP TO THE WOODEN GATE OF THE CAMP SPONSORED BY THE Compulsivity Clinics of America, after having been dropped off in the parking lot by a friend, I felt my stomach knot in fear. *Don't be silly,* I told myself. *You're here to learn more about yourself—why you've been a compulsive person all your life. There is nothing to be afraid of.*

I'd felt this way before—the first day of school . . . being dropped off at a Girl Scout camp. But to have these feelings now was ridiculous. I was forty-eight years old!

Anxiously I looked about the crowded parking lot—doors

slamming, men and women tugging suitcases and duffle bags from yawning car trunks. Were all these people as apprehensive as I?

A ruddy-faced young man standing in the center of the parking lot pointed up a blacktop path toward a gray wooden lodge half-hidden in the Minnesota woods. Falling oak leaves swirled about his head as he spoke. "You'll be staying up there at the end of the path. Down here"—he gestured at a brown log building closer by—"is where you get fed."

A comforting thought, being fed. Was I going to be preoccupied with food this week?

Only a month ago my interest had been perked by a telephone conversation with a vivacious young woman who had just "graduated" from this Compulsivity Clinic course. She had enrolled with serious food disorders only to discover she was alcoholic as well.

I knew I had been an alcoholic—correction, was a recovering alcoholic—and that I had other compulsive behavior problems as well. It was time to subdue the rest of these monsters.

The advance information had fascinated me:

The Compulsivity Clinic program offers you the opportunity to uncover the causes of your compulsive behaviors. It provides support to make lifestyle changes. You will learn about:

Addictive relationships
Managing change
Dealing with shame and guilt
Chemical dependencies
Sexual abuse and addiction

Self-defeating lifestyle problems can include:

Workaholism
Relationship dependency
Eating disorders
Smoking
Gambling

As I struggled up the walkway with my suitcase, I was filled with fresh resolve to uncover those hidden areas buried deep within myself. Dread and exhilaration coursed through my veins, unlikely companions.

At the door of the lodge a staff member issued a green plastic three-ring notebook containing the week's schedule and other information, then with a warm smile assigned me to a bed. All the staff people looked energetic, lean, disciplined, bright. I wondered how they viewed us.

What are these people going to find out about me?

More terrifyingly: *What am I going to find out about myself?*

The women's sleeping areas were separated by carpeted room dividers. I found my cubicle at the far end on the right side. Good. I'd have some privacy here. Suddenly I wanted to protect myself from getting too close to these others.

Across the aisle I glimpsed a thin young woman solemnly unpacking an orange nylon duffle bag, methodically and mechanically sorting her personal belongings. A pile of paperback books slid onto the floor with a thud. As she dove to retrieve them, the words *child abuse* on one of the covers caught my eye.

I could only speculate that my silent roommate across the way bore some invisible scars.

After tidying up my tiny cubicle, I looked it over with satisfaction. To counter harsh ceiling lights, I had brought my small gooseneck reading lamp. It now threw a comforting beam of light on my "security blanket"—a new blue down bathrobe, a recent purchase so I would not be cold in the Minnesota night air.

At five o'clock we all streamed back to the brown log dining hall for an early dinner. I fought down nervousness as I filled my plate and selected a seat. *You've been in groups before,* I told myself. *Relax.*

It was a futile command. The thick hero sandwich I began to stuff into my mouth suddenly exploded into a shower of ham, lettuce, tomato, and onions. As I tried to catch the falling food, my paper plate tumbled to the floor. My feet were awash in debris.

As every eye in the room turned to survey the mess, I let out a self-conscious giggle. Immediately the entire room broke into gales of laughter.

"Looks like you'd better start all over again," cracked a large blonde woman seated next to me. As she turned toward me, I noticed a steel brace supporting her back.

Looking around the room at the now-smiling faces, I felt cheered somehow that my blunder had been a welcome icebreaker. Everyone had been as tense as I was.

After dinner the leadership team was introduced, including Terry Kellogg, founder of the Compulsivity Clinics, and we got down to basics. First some important definitions were explained to us.

Obsession: recurring, persistent thoughts, images, or impulses that occur in your mind. They seem to come from nowhere; they are not voluntary. You do not seem to be able to control or suppress them, though you try.

Compulsion: an insistent, repetitive, intrusive, and unwanted urge to perform an act that is contrary to one's ordinary wishes or standards. Since it serves as a defensive substitute for even more unacceptable unconscious ideas or wishes, failure to perform the compulsive act leads to anxiety. Performing it relieves anxiety. Yet performing it is also linked with the desire to resist doing it and often a sense of shame. The compulsive link to a particular act, event, experience (like gambling or shopping), or thing (like alcohol) often leads to addiction.

Addiction: a pathological link or relationship with a mood-altering act, event, experience, or thing that causes major life problems. An addiction is more serious than a compulsion and can be life-threatening if it involves substance abuse (alcohol, drugs, or even food and tobacco). It is behavior that continues despite adverse emotional, medical, financial, or social consequences.

After the introductory staff comments, the twenty-five of us who had enrolled in the Clinic introduced ourselves and spoke briefly about the problems that had brought us there. We were alcoholics, drug addicts, chain-smokers, gamblers, compulsive TV-watchers. Many had come with sexual compulsions or severe relationship dependencies. Most of us had one form of eating disorder or another. Some were given to excessive shopping, spending, or other types of binge behaviors. It was heartening, somehow, to know that my secrets, my problems, were also the secrets and problems of others. Several faces now became brightened by a new sense of hope.

Mic Hunter (who is now the coordinator of the Clinic) assured us that what seemed impossible to resist was indeed resistible, that our problems were treatable and curable. He was later to offer this checklist to help identify compulsive behaviors:

- Is the behavior ritualized? If interrupted, does the person get upset?

- Is there time distortion when the person is involved in this behavior? (Does it go on for much longer than he thinks it does or than he expects?)

- Does the person set rigid rules for himself in this behavior, and then tend to violate them? (He says he'll drink only between the hours of ten and twelve, and then doesn't; etc.)

- Does the person go to extremes, from overdoing to underdoing, in this behavior?

- If there are negative consequences, does the person continue the behavior anyway?

- Is there any "situation stressor" causing this behavior? (A man insulted sexually by a woman who has spurned him, for instance, may launch a succession of promiscuous relationships, but only to prove his masculinity and not as a compulsive behavior. When he understands the reason for what she said, or that it isn't true, he will stop his promiscuity.)

- Is there preoccupation ("obsessing") about this behavior, in which the person thinks more about it than anything else, so that it interferes with his life? (Copyright © 1986 by Mic Hunter; taken from the forthcoming *Excessive Appetites*.)

After the introductory comments, our first group session came in a small room with mahogany-paneled walls and one large window. We all sat on floor pillows. It felt strangely cozy inside these walls, almost womblike. There we met our six group members: two men and four women, including myself.

Our counselor, Maureen, welcomed us: "You are to become a family—to eat together, spend time together when we are not in this room, and 'be there' for each other. I want you to experience trust and love for one another, something you may never have really known in your own families."

She paused a moment. "For the rest of the week please do not contact anyone on the outside. This is especially important for those of you with relationship dependencies. We suggest you don't call out and 'get a fix.' You're here to focus on yourselves, to feel your true feelings and confront your fears. I urge you to stay within the framework of our program so as not to become fragmented."

I liked Maureen, a lovely Irish wisp of a woman with a cloud of short auburn hair and a mellow, soothing voice that was competent and reassuring. Maureen described herself as a recovering alcoholic from a strongly "dysfunctional" family.

"Over ninety percent of American families are dysfunctional to some degree," she added. She defined the dysfunctional family as one in which either father or mother or child has a problem that causes an imbalance in family relationships. A father may be addicted to alcohol; a mother may have a nervous breakdown; a son or daughter may have a serious illness. Whatever the specific issue, the family begins to revolve around the problem, ceasing to function in a healthy, mutually supportive way.

Soon a cover-up of feelings begins. Hurt, angry, confused emotions are stuffed down inside of us, kept concealed even from ourselves. Out-of-touch with our own deepest truth, we feel driven to do things without knowing why. Compulsive behavior is born.

Fred, a heavy-set man in his thirties, sat in the corner frowning. He was a stockbroker in the Gamblers Anonymous program. Wall Street, he confided, was spawning a new breed of gambler, the compulsive investor. Fred spoke slowly, as though physically exhausted.

Maureen bore in on him. "I suspect you are so full of sugar and starch—they act as a medication, you know—that your real feelings can't get through. For the rest of your time here, Fred, I want you to totally abstain from all sugar and white flour. You need to cleanse your body of these substances before you can start to *feel* what you need to feel."

The stories that poured out from this group triggered memories and pain of my own:

"I've always had problems with money and men."

"I'm a chain-smoker and addicted to soap operas."

"My wife said if I didn't get some help for my pornography addiction she would divorce me."

"My father raped me when I was eight; then my uncle and my two brothers took advantage of me. I hate them all."

My contribution: "I've had five years of sobriety, but I know I've only struck the tip of the iceberg in working out my compulsive behavior."

Each person spoke with deep emotion, some with anger, some with tears. An ever-present box of tissues was scooted about the room. Complete strangers a few hours earlier, we began to see ourselves by the end of the session as being bound by a common thread of inner pain.

I was too keyed up after this encounter to go to bed, so I took a short walk under the trees. Geese honked on nearby Lake Minnetonka; the smell of burning leaves recalled fall nights in Vermont where I grew up.

I wondered about how I had come across. Had I sounded too "put together"? Hollow? Superficial? Defensive? Had I used too many humorous quips to keep people from getting too close—because I was too selfish or scared to communicate more meaningfully?

After breakfast the next morning I stopped to talk with the woman in the steel back brace who had sat next to me the night before at dinner. Perched uncomfortably on a straight naugahyde chair, she was wheezing and struggling for breath.

"Can I help you?" I offered weakly.

She pointed to her pack of cigarettes. "You could take these things and throw them in the lake. But I'd probably be fool enough to dive in after them."

"I used to be hooked on them, too," I said, then wondered if my "used to" sounded lofty or self-righteous.

The morning small group session was heavy going. We again sat on pillows in a circle, while Steve, the other male in our group, sobbed uncontrollably and rocked back and forth on his pillow. He told the group about his problem.

"I hate myself!" he kept saying, pounding at the oversized pillow beneath him. "I told myself when I came here I wouldn't read that stuff again, but I did last night before I went to bed. Then I took a fantasy trip and. . . ." He didn't go on.

"Steve, who are you *really* angry at?" Maureen asked.

He was silent for a moment. "I guess it's my parents. It goes 'way back. As kids, we couldn't be normal. You know, no smoking, no drinking, no dancing, no movies."

"So reading sex magazines was a way to get back at them," ventured Maureen.

Steve nodded. "The only thing my parents ever said to me about sex was, 'Don't do it. It's wrong.' Since they wouldn't answer my questions about masturbation, I felt like a freak." He started to pound his thighs with his fists.

"Steve, stop beating yourself up," Maureen ordered. "I want you to get in touch with how lonely you have been, how isolated you've felt."

Steve's realization moments later: "When I started rebelling, voices inside me began saying, 'You're *bad*!' That really scared me. I guess I was scared because I wondered if those voices in my head were from my parents or from God or from the pit of hell."

He talked for a half hour. We all went through his torment with him. Finally spent from this wrenching session, Steve leaned back against the wall. The toes of his stained white tennis shoes were tilted slightly inward, reminding me of a little boy abandoned in his playpen. I had a glimpse then of a little Steve, desperate and lonely, wanting to be picked up and held.

Then the little boy opened his eyes, reached for his horn-rimmed glasses, cleared his throat, and was transformed before our compassionate eyes into the Steve of today, the forty-year-old accountant.

Each day there was some kind of breakthrough in a member of our group. Some of the things I heard resembled my own nightmares. Others represented the secrets and fears of other lives.

Peggy, thirtyish, with green eyes and a sprinkle of freckles, was office manager for a small insurance company. Despite her responsible position, she had come to the Clinic desperately needy and scared. The oldest girl in a family of four, she'd been responsible for the care of her younger brothers and sisters. Her mother, obese and deeply disturbed emotionally, had spent most of her time in bed, getting up only for trips to the bathroom or refrigerator. Her father, a violent and abusive man, had beaten his children unmercifully.

"I became sexually active with boys in my class at age thirteen," Peggy related. "By the time I was seventeen, I'd tried it all except marriage. That was a disaster. All four of my marriages have been failures. I've lost track of the times I've tried to kill myself—six, eight."

"Why suicide?" asked Maureen.

"Maybe suicide was an attempt to kill that part of me I didn't like. The guiltiest I feel is about my abortion twelve years ago. Since my marriage was breaking up, I thought it would be a mistake to bring a child into the world. I never told my husband."

"Would you like to let go of that guilt, Peggy?" Maureen asked.

Peggy wiped her nose with the back of her hand. "Oh, God, *yes*! Is there any way I can?"

Maureen moved across the room to where Peggy was sitting and put her arm around her. "We're going to have a memorial service for your child, right here. Would you like to invite the group to be part of it?"

Peggy blinked, her stricken eyes meeting the gaze of each of us seated around the room. "Would you all like to come?" she asked.

Profoundly affected, we nodded.

What Maureen didn't tell us then is that ritual acts often help to break the pattern of guilt that underlies compulsive behavior. That is why cleansing rituals as an expression of real faith—rituals like baptism and communion—play such an important role in many addicts' recovery.

"Does your daughter have a name, Peggy?" Maureen asked.

"Yes. Her name is Kim."

"Please invite Kim to come into the room and be with us now."

Peggy moved her lips self-consciously, her eyes filling with tears.

"Would you describe Kim to all of us, Peggy?"

"She is twelve years old. Her hair is blonde and she has blue eyes. She looks so sad. There are tears in her eyes. . . ."

"Do you know why she looks so sad, Peggy? It's because she doesn't want you to go on mourning for her. She is happy and at peace in heaven. Is there anything you'd like to say to Kim?"

Breaking a long pause, Peggy blurted in a shaking voice, *"Please forgive me, Kim. I was so confused when I found out I was pregnant with you. I was so frightened and unhappy. I didn't dare to have you . . . please forgive me!*

"I love you, Kim. I miss you and I miss not having you with me now when I could be a mom to you. But I wasn't ready. I hope you can understand that." Peggy broke down, her tears and mascara running together down her cheeks. Most of the women in the group were also weeping.

"Is there anything else you want to say to her, Peggy?"

"Just I love you . . . I love you . . . I know we will be together someday. . . ."

"It's time to say good-bye to her, to let her go."

"Good-bye, Kim . . . good-bye . . . I love you. . . ."

The six days with the Clinic felt like forever, yet when it was over they seemed to have sped by. We had exercise sessions, lectures on the dysfunctional family, sexual disorders, nutrition, and so forth. Information helps us to get a handle on our problems, I learned, because fear plays a major role in compulsive behavior.

The last morning I took an early morning walk alone, past Lake Minnetonka into the forest. The woods were pungent with the smell of moist earth. I found a sunny spot on a gently sloping hill where leaves protected me from the damp ground. Easing my body to the ground, I looked skyward in self-examination. I felt strangely vulnerable, so I began a deep breathing exercise we had been taught in one of our sessions. In . . . out . . . in . . . out. We had been taught that getting proper oxygen to the brain is often enough to help reduce or eliminate the fear response. Agoraphobics and other people afflicted with fear are often able to reduce their anxiety simply by improved breathing. Hyperventilation occurs frequently during anxiety attacks and makes you feel dizzy, that you are losing control.

The breathing exercise helps compulsives as well. We used it in combination with focusing mentally on our grief, pain, or sadness. After a while a surge of emotion welled up from deep inside me. I sobbed wrenching sobs, thinking of my new friends. The intimate details of our lives we had shared, and the mutual support we had given one another, had brought us close together.

The Compulsivity Clinic had provided insights into the nature of the problem millions of women face, but left me with unanswered questions: How can compulsive people change? Were we wounded ones permanently damaged or was there a clearly marked path to wholeness? How far along was I? Were there any positive elements in compulsive behavior?

The root cause of all compulsions, we had been told, was fear and shame. I needed to ponder that deeply, to look for the origins of shame in my own background.

The search would take me not only into my own history, but into the experiences of many others. It would take me to hospitals and clinics, halfway houses and self-help groups, into libraries and research centers. It would set me interviewing health professionals and people struggling with current addictions.

I offer my own story following as an illustration of the genesis and growth of compulsive behavior. It is typical of the inhibiting and self-defeating patterns many women live and suffer under. It also illustrates the process by which you and I can be released from the bondage in which compulsions keep us.

2

The Violated Childhood

More than other emotions, shame involves a quality of the unexpected; if in any way we feel it coming we are powerless to avert it. This is in part because of the difficulty we have in admitting to ourselves either shame or the circumstances that give rise to shame. Whatever part voluntary action may have in the experience of shame is swallowed up in the sense of something that overwhelms us from without and 'takes us' unawares. We are taken by surprise, caught off guard, or off base, caught unawares, made a fool of. It is as if we were suddenly invaded from the rear where we cannot see, are unprotected, and can be overpowered.

Helen Merrell Lynd
On Shame and the Search for Identity

*I*LEARNED SOMETHING ABOUT MYSELF FROM EVERY PERSON AT THE CLINIC. Some of their experiences helped me open long-closed doors in my past. Peggy's story was much sadder and more traumatic than mine but, her green eyes clouded, she pried open a door I had sealed shut in my childhood. Peggy traced her low self-worth to unremitting abusive treatment by her father, and the unsupporting, passive behavior of her obese mother, who became a negative role model for her.

Because her mother was so disturbed, Peggy had to fill the role of mother to the other children. Before she reached puberty, Peggy found a way to prevent her father from beating his children: sex. If she gave in to her father's demands, he would not abuse the younger children.

"My father wanted to have sex with me all the time. I just didn't have the strength to resist, so I let him," Peggy had told us dispassionately. "I felt it was my fault somehow that my mother acted so strangely."

My heart had ached for her. Basically a talented, responsible person—she'd held her office job for seven years—Peggy's emotional life was a mess. A compulsive eater and drinker, obsessed by fears, she had been looking desperately for help. The memorial service for her aborted child, Kim, had been a good start. A lot more healing had to take place inside Peggy before she could acquire positive feelings about herself.

What was the connection, I wondered, between sexual abuse in childhood and compulsive behavior problems in adulthood?

Reading *Silent Scream* by Martha Janssen on her incestuous relationship with her father helped me understand Peggy's agony of spirit. Martha Janssen's book is written in blank verse:

> *Daughters love to sit*
> *on daddies' laps.*
> *Me too.*
> *I would scramble up*
> *at the end of the day.*
> *We'd talk until Mother left the room.*
> *Then we'd "play."*
>
> *Now I know*
> *why I watch so carefully*
> *little girls sitting*
> *on their daddies' laps.*

Then this indictment addressed to her abusive father:

> *You!*
> *You walk calmly*
> *among people, relatives.*
> *They don't know you*
> *as I do.*
> *You smile*
> *and feel no guilt*
>   *no shame.*
> *You walk away from my pain.*
>
> *This is crazy.*
> *I carry the weight of the sentence*
> *But you are the killer.*[1]

My mind went back to a clinic lecture. If children are sexually molested, then the "boundaries" of their bodies have been violated. It's as though their right to say no has been stolen from them. Thus they grow up confused, with certain protective limits erased, prone to erratic and compulsive behavior. Such people have a lifelong struggle with shame.

Shame, I learned, has to do with how we feel about ourselves, whereas guilt has to do with our behavior. We incur guilt when we violate some value we hold, but it has a constructive purpose in that it motivates us to make amends. Shame has no such constructive purpose, in that it turns us away from others and strikes a blow at our very worth as persons. Shame isolates, alienates. It makes us feel we're no good, that we're unworthy of respect.

Because shame is almost impossible to communicate, and because a person suffering from shame tends not to talk about his problem—or even perhaps be aware of it—he looks for temporary relief through some outlet like food, drugs, or alcohol, any "mood-alterer" to ease his pain.

An estimated seventy percent of all women who come to treatment centers are victims of sexual abuse as children. Estimates of sexual abuse of girls under fourteen range from 45,000 to 500,000 incidents per year. Some estimate that one in every four girls and one in six boys in the U.S. will be sexually molested before they are eighteen. Government statistics, moreover, indicate that nearly fifty percent are victimized by a member of their own family. The *Ms.* study (see page 11) compiled striking anecdotal evidence that "women who have been victims of incest or rape are vastly overrepresented among the addicted population."

Only in recent years have women been able to acknowledge their rejected memories and describe their experiences. The emotional progression of a victim goes something like this:[2]

1. Deep inner hurt and dismay over the sexual violation; a feeling of being damaged goods.

2. Fearful resolve not to tell anyone.

3. An attempt to bury the episode(s) in one's subconscious, where the memory festers and creates an inner disorder.

4. Adult relationships with men are damaged.

5. Trust and intimacy problems with both sexes develop.

6. Suicide can seem the answer—as it had to Peggy.

   The road back to health for the victim takes this course:

1. Facing up to the fact of abuse, dredging it up from the subconscious.

2. In a therapeutic setting, admitting to others that it happened, as Peggy did in our small group. Once this exposure gets the abuse into the light, much of the destructive power goes out of it.

3. Seeing it as the abuser's problem and fault, not the victim's.

4. Forgiving him/her for it.

Peggy's experience, outwardly so different from my own, nevertheless had triggered childhood memories. The change from the emotionally charged atmosphere of the six-day Compulsivity Clinic to the more relaxed pace in my small rural community was what I needed to begin to sort them out. I developed a whole new perspective on this period of my life, including one traumatic episode that had burst out of my subconscious. One day with notepad and pen I began to dig into my early years.

At first glance my childhood seemed utterly normal. An only child, I was reared in the small community of St. Johnsbury Center, Vermont. My father, Richard Simpson, was a handsome and gregarious man, and served as a salesman, first for an appliance store, later for an automobile dealer. His wife, Elizabeth, my mother, was a fragile, pretty woman who centered her life on homemaking with few outside interests.

For me going to the old Congregational village church was a high point. On Sunday mornings I'd arrive starched and curled, eager for the Sunday school lesson to begin. The smells linger to this day; men's minty aftershave, the musky, damp odor of the church bell rope (how I longed to give it a hearty tug), coffee, cinnamon, and ham from the church kitchen.

I can still see the ladies dressed in dotted swiss and print voile dresses, their "finger-waved" hair-dos precise as metal washboards. The men in their three-piece suits seemed oddly stiff, as though their legs wouldn't bend in pants with such razor-sharp creases. Their hair slicked down with Brilliantine, noses and cheeks aglow from vigorous scrubbing, their hearty "how-do-you-do's" rang through the building.

My classroom was a clutter of small oak chairs presided over by our teacher, my Aunt Ethel. Next to the large blackboard was an oak-framed picture of Jesus. I recall his strong, sensitive face, long, beautiful, flowing hair—and those eyes. Warm, loving eyes. Jesus was holding the lost sheep in one arm, a staff in the other hand, a red cape over his long white garment.

"Jesus loves you," Aunt Ethel would intone. "He wants you to come to him with whatever is bothering you." What was bothering me in those early years was the fact that my father and mother didn't seem to love each other as other daddies and mommies did, but I couldn't even tell Jesus this.

Then my aunt would teach us from the Bible. A verse she often chose was, "He was wounded for our transgressions, he was bruised for our iniquities . . . and with his stripes we are healed."[3] I couldn't understand these words at all. Aunt Ethel explained that the stripes were the wounds of Christ, but the only wounds I saw in the picture books were in his hands and feet. They looked more like holes in his flesh than stripes. Yet the verse was strangely comforting.

The hour of Bible stories always passed too quickly for me. Soon it was time to join the grown-ups in the auditorium, where the organist extracted loud and wondrous sounds from the quaking mahogany organ with her favorite selection: "Yes, Jesus loves me. . . ."

How I loved these Sunday afternoons when we'd motor around the Vermont countryside in our slate-gray 1938 Plymouth! Occasionally we'd take the hour's journey to where my Uncle Ralph and Aunt Agnes lived. Aunt Agnes always had freshly fried doughnuts and orange Kool-Aid for us, and her house smelled of lavender and polished wood.

One of these visits, however, was not so pleasant. For many years what happened that Sunday at Uncle Ralph's had lain buried deep inside me. Peggy helped me recall it. The rest I discovered in a therapy session. As I began to put the episode down on paper, I trembled so violently I had to get out of my chair and walk around the room.

It happened when I was five. On this particular Sunday we had driven there in time for lunch. Afterward we gathered around the old player piano in the living room for a songfest. Uncle Ralph let me select the music roll from the glass-front cabinet where the player rolls were stored, then sit beside him on the piano bench.

Mother and Aunt Agnes didn't sing, just sat nearby smiling encouragingly as Dad, Uncle Ralph, and I warbled away. Dad sang tenor to Uncle Ralph's bass, with my squeaky child's voice feebly carrying the melody.

Every time a polka was played, I'd slip off the bench and skip about the house, through the dark hall with its ticking clocks, past Uncle Ralph's gun case with the stuffed animals on top, then out through the kitchen past the black wrought-iron stove with its gleaming chrome trim, on into the dining room. Breathless, I'd bound back onto the piano bench, bumping affectionately into Uncle Ralph as he manipulated the brass levers beside the keyboard.

When the music ended, Aunt Agnes, a gardener of great skill, invited us to help pick vegetables for dinner. Usually when she suggested this I'd be the first one out the door, but on this occasion I decided to stay behind while Uncle Ralph rolled his handmade cigarettes, a ritual I found fascinating. All the ingredients were in place to start production when Uncle Ralph sank down into his oak rocking chair. I noticed that his face was flushed and his breathing wheezy.

"Is something wrong, Uncle Ralph?" I asked.

"No, dear, not really, but I would feel better if you'd come over here and sit on my lap."

Eager to please, I approached the seated figure, turning my back to him expecting to be lifted into his lap. Instead his strong hands pressed my small body next to him. He gripped so tightly I could hardly breathe; then one hand groped for my pubic area. I heard his rasping, measured breath, felt the brass fittings on his suspenders digging into my shoulders.

What was going on? Why was he breathing so fast? Now he was pressing and poking and hurting me through my cotton dress.

Terror filled me. Shame . . . horror. What if Dad and Mom and Aunt Agnes were to walk in now? I could hear their voices chatting nonchalantly outside. "Let's dig some more beets," I heard my father say.

What is this man whom I love and trust doing to me? Uncle Ralph wouldn't touch me *there*. . . . But he is, and he's acting crazy and frantic and his false teeth are clicking in my ears. Oh, somebody help me!

Little short gasps and moans, then his hands dropped limply beside me. He slumped back in the squeaking rocker like an exhausted rag doll, his eyes shut, the spittle running down the corners of his mouth. The only sound now was the *tick-tock* of the hall clocks.

Breaking loose from his locked legs, I streaked upstairs to the bathroom, past the stuffed animals, my heart pounding, my stomach heaving, my eyes burning with tears of guilt and fright. There was the beautiful ceramic jar with the blue forget-me-nots where Aunt Agnes saved the long strands of her jet-black hair. This saintly and pristine lady, what would she think of me? I let Uncle Ralph touch those private parts that Mother told me no one was to see or touch. Mother and Dad would be furious if they knew! They must never find out. Deep within me something was dying—a joyfulness and a trust. A passage had been made from innocence to something I wasn't quite sure of, something frightening and unclean.

I pressed my body so hard against the washbasin that my chest ached. Gallons of water must have passed through my desperately scrubbing hands. My nightmare was interrupted by a familiar tap at the door. My dad always knocked that way. *Dum-dum-da-dum-dum—da-dum.*

Poking his head around the door, he teased, "Snookie, are you going to use up all the water in the reservoir? We're waiting on you to come help with dinner."

"I'll be right down, Daddy."

Shyly I entered the kitchen, the skipping child of an hour ago now silent, ashamed, wounded by an encounter she neither understood nor could share. Irrevocably I gave myself an order: *I will never ever tell anyone what happened today.*

The beets stained my small fingers as I scrubbed off the dirt in the old stainless steel sink. My hands were almost raw. Would I ever feel clean again?

Years later at the Compulsivity Clinic, I asked Mic Hunter if this single instance of sexual abuse could be one of the underlying causes of my compulsive behavior.

Compulsivity, he admitted, usually has a complicated genesis. The shame/guilt reaction of the victim in cases of abuse can be a major contributing factor. The key is the way in which the family responds to the person who has been victimized. In my case, he said, there was no one I felt I could talk to. Nor did anyone notice my trauma symptoms. The implication to me as a child was: *Your pain doesn't matter.* So I forced the pain inward and blamed myself.

It was significant, I think, that I tried ritual obsessive hand-washing to cleanse myself.

According to psychologists Pamela Vredevelt and Kathryn Rodriguez in their book *Surviving the Secret,* there are five common identity and interpersonal problems suffered by sexual abuse victims:

1. Minimizing their own abilities and maximizing others' strengths.

2. Tending to take responsibility for others' behavior.

3. Having difficulty achieving intimacy with others.

4. Tending to think if they please others they will be considered "perfect."

5. Worrying obsessively about problems and sabotaging their own efforts to change.

In retrospect, I can see that my experience of being abused shattered not only the trust I had in myself, but also in others close to me—and even of the boundaries of the world as I knew it.

3

The Dysfunctional Home

Passive dependent people are so busy seeking to be loved that they have no energy left to love. They are like starving people, scrounging wherever they can for food, and with no food of their own to give to others. It is as if within them they have an inner emptiness, a bottomless pit crying out to be filled but which can never be completely filled.

M. Scott Peck, M.D.
The Road Less Traveled

*T*HOUGH I WAS FORTUNATE THAT NEITHER OF MY PARENTS DRANK—I became an alcoholic in spite of this—it was apparent to me at an early age that my father and mother did not enjoy being with one another. Dad's absence for three years during World War II didn't help. Our home, off-balance because of the problem relationship between my two parents, was dysfunctional.

As the alienation between my mother and father grew, a spirit of sadness took over our home. A dome of silence seemed to settle over us. Yet for years, probably because of me, their only child, my parents struggled to hold their marriage together.

I remember a recurring dream in which I was a lifeguard trying to pull my parents to the ocean's shore. I'd swim frantically to rescue one as the other went under. I could never get them both to safety; one or the other would drown before I could reach him. Choices! Which one to save? Why couldn't I save them both? I'd awaken tangled in my bedclothes, heart pounding, my nightgown soaked in perspiration.

Tensely I'd lie awake until my dad's short, dry cough from the adjoining bedroom, and the sound of Mother's steady breathing, assured me that all was well.

But all was not well. They were playing a charade called marriage. Sometimes my mind would form a strange fantasy. I'd imagine that our rambling three-story house was actually made of cardboard. If you cut on the dotted line you could fold it up and return it to the carton it had come in. One day I'd return home from school and there would be nothing there—just a grassy plot with a few lilac bushes standing sentinel over an empty hole.

Often my heart would race with fear as I hurried up the broken asphalt sidewalk of Elm Street after school. Maybe today was the day the house had vanished. All the other neat clapboard homes were in place, their prim, Priscilla-curtained windows following my anxious odyssey toward home. Eagerly my eyes would sweep up the street to our house on the hill. It was still there!

My steps would quicken. I hoped there would be a simmering pot of chowder on the stove. First I stamped my muddy feet on the square raffia mat, then burst into the kitchen. I was always trying to bring light and sunshine into the house, into my parents' cold marriage.

There was Mother, neatly groomed in her modest cotton house dress, her sad hazel eyes lighting up as her only child came through the door. She seemed so fragile, so vulnerable. I felt responsible for her. How I wanted to throw my arms around her and tell her not to worry, that I would protect her.

After chowder and cookies I would slip out the kitchen door and head for my very own sanctuary. There it was! The golden glow of the afternoon burst through the pink-and-white blossoms of my apple tree, warming my long braids and sprinkling me with diamonds. My skin was dusted with golden flecks of light. The red clover and buttercups in my hand were celestial blooms.

Vermont disappeared in a misty vapor, our house and garage spinning away into space. Here I was away from sad people, unhappy people. My apple tree was a magic place. There was no pain here. No confusion. No one spoke cross or accusing words.

My tree always welcomed me. It never said, "Come back later; I have branches to straighten now." Just, "Come rest in my arms. You're safe here."

My tree had a heartbeat. I could feel the rhythm pulsating as I sat in the branches. I didn't mind sharing my tree with the robins and the fat honeybees.

My earliest "addiction" was for love and approval. There were happy times with my father. He taught me while I was still small to use carpentry tools and do other boyish things. I was only four when I started "helping" him work on our gray Plymouth. He'd take the motor apart, placing nuts and bolts and gaskets in murky baths of lubricating oil. I'd swirl them around with my hands and squeal in delight as the oil ran down my arms. How much I depended on Daddy's approval!

Knowing deep down that my parents' marriage was failing, I tried harder to please. It was at this point that I slipped into what I now know as the "co-dependent role." I so wanted our family life to be happy that I was ready to play any part that could bring this about. Very early, perhaps as a contrast to the joylessness in our home, I determined to be a "fun person." I was always playing jokes on others, mimicking my teachers and friends. I laughed a lot, developed a reputation as a class clown. I was not yet a true compulsive, but already my gaiety had something excessive about it, as though I were telling myself, "I *will* be happy!" Hurting inside, my defense was a perpetual smile.

Years later I was to read my own youthful situation reflected in the words of social philosopher Helen Lynd: "The discovery that our parents are not all-wise and all-good and that we must face the uncertainties of our own judgment . . . is a lonely experience. It becomes still more lonely and poignant, and in a real sense shameful, when it is followed by a realization that, instead of our elders being our interpreters of the world, our protectors, we must, instead, protect them from their own fallibilities and shortcomings, and from the shameful knowledge that we are aware of them" (*On Shame and the Search for Identity*).

I was also to learn that an addiction-prone personality like mine typically manifests an exaggerated degree of compliance, and is overly concerned with pleasing people and winning approval.

But not even my desperately cheerful facade, as it turned out, could stop the breakup of our home. I was fifteen when Mother and Dad separated and filed for divorce. I retreated to my apple tree on the hill. By now my teenage legs were too long for the "stirrup" limbs and it seemed pretty dumb to sit in a tree at my age. So I'd lean up against the warm bark, feeling the heartbeat of the moving sap. Was my parents' separation something I had caused? Was there something I could still do?

All year my heart throbbed like a toothache. Typical of young people in dysfunctional families, I felt increasingly responsible to take care of my mother. To fix everything in her life, to "make it all better"—the phrase she'd often used when she kissed a bump or scratch.

My tree had no answers. So I retreated behind an air of bravado, masking my hurt with a casual veneer. Life was a charade . . . smile . . . pretend. I practiced my act before my dressing table mirror— "so-what" expressions, "I-couldn't-care-less" gestures. Cultivate the quick, merry laugh, Sandra Jean. Crinkle your eyes in merriment.

After the divorce both my parents entered second marriages that proved to be solid and lasting. Not aware of the happiness ahead for them, however, I remained the confused child in-between. Feeling disconnected with family life, I sought love like candy, and tried intensely to be more acceptable to my friends.

One of these friends was Linette. She was a sunny blonde with a dazzling smile and a Bo Derek figure that drove the guys at Spaulding High School wild. We were sophomores when Linette invited me to spend the weekend with her while her parents were away in Montreal.

She set out popcorn and potato chips, then poured Cokes from a frosty twelve-ounce bottle. "Should we put some bourbon in these?" she asked.

"That would be fine with me!" I replied in my best Rita Hayworth imitation. I had never seen a bottle of bourbon.

Linette went to a dining room cabinet and flung open the double doors. Before us stood a dazzling array of liquor—vodka, gin, Scotch, bourbon, brandy, wine, creme de menthe, rum, champagne. What an education!

How worldly I suddenly felt, as she measured a crystal shot glass of bourbon into each glass of Coke. After stirring the swirling mixture with a pink flamingo swizzle stick, she triumphantly handed me my glass.

"Here's to Spaulding High!" she toasted.

The mossy smell of the liquor sifted through the sweet Coke aroma. Now I was in the big leagues—a rite of passage—a woman at last!

Yuk. The first rush of bubbly liquid hit my tongue. "This tastes awful, Linette."

"It gets better as you go along," she assured me.

Sure enough, the second and third swallows were less pungent. A warm, tingly feeling was taking hold. "I see what you mean. This is okay!" I burbled, gulping the contents of the glass.

"Hey, take it easy," Linette warned. "You shouldn't drink it so fast!"

Before long my body felt as though it were floating in warm butterscotch sauce. I felt cozy and cared for. Cared about.

"Do you suppose I could have another?" I don't remember how many times I asked this question that evening.

Sometime later Linette telephoned our boyfriends. When it came my turn to talk, I gushed something wonderfully witty into the phone.

"You all right, Sandy?" the boy on the line asked. "You sound funny."

That's the last thing I remember.

I awakened fully clothed, flat on my back in Linette's guest room bed. By flinging my leg over the side, I stopped the room from spinning. Then waves of nausea came and I rushed for the bathroom. Kneeling on the tile floor I gripped the toilet in a death lock.

I didn't feel at all like Rita Hayworth now.

It would be two years before I had another drink . . . but I had the exact chemistry to become an alcoholic. I see myself in this statement: "The dulling of sensibility, the soothing feeling that all is well, is a powerful experience for some people. . . . Those who depend totally on such an experience do so because it gives their lives a structure and secures them, at least subjectively, against the press of what is novel and demanding. This is what they are addicted to" (Dr. Stanton Peele in *Love and Addiction*).

After graduating from high school, I enrolled at the Rhode Island School of Design in Providence. Weekends several of us would go to nearby Brown University for fraternity house weekend parties. Feeling like a small-town bumpkin in my homemade clothes, unsure of myself in the company of sophisticated Ivy League girls, I began to depend on alcohol for my security.

During exam week in May 1956, at the end of my second year in Rhode Island, I got a telephone call from my father who was now living in Barre, Vermont, with his new wife, Nora. "The Chamber of Commerce wants Barre to have a contestant in the Miss Vermont Pageant this year," he told me, "so I volunteered you. Your picture ran in last night's paper."

I was too stunned to speak. Dad had always been a practical joker, but this time he'd gone too far.

"The pageant is next weekend at the Burlington High School Auditorium," he continued. "You'll need to be there on Friday with a talent presentation."

Panic set in even before I hung up. What would I wear? What in the world could I do for a talent presentation? Could I lose twenty pounds before next weekend? Fretful hazel eyes stared back at me from the bathroom mirror. Dark circles. Jowls. Why did I stuff myself with all those sugar doughnuts at the Bluebird Cafe?

Somehow I completed my exams, got some clothes together, and made the trip to Burlington, Vermont, all in three days' time. The pageant weekend activities were a blur of teas, lunches, interviews, and rehearsals. The night of the finals was brutally hot; the makeshift fans that wheezed asthmatically from the gymnasium balcony raised barely a tickle of breeze. As I went onstage to do my talent, I was sure I would faint.

I'd decided to repeat a skit I'd done at the School of Design, a pantomime about the precocious little six-year-old Eloise who lived in New York's Plaza Hotel. To my amazement the audience in Vermont seemed to like it: riotous laughter and applause.

Still, as the contestants circled the stifling auditorium in formal gowns for the final time, I knew I had no chance of winning in the face of the far more beautiful and talented competition. I was already undressing in the basement as the announcer began to call up to the stage the runners-up for the title of Miss Vermont.

I had just gotten out of my soggy copper-colored velvet gown and was struggling with a jammed hook and eye on my voluminous crinoline hoopskirt when the final announcement came: *"And now, Miss Vermont of 1956, Sandra Jean Simpson of Barre!"*

I couldn't be hearing right.

Struggling back into my clothes, I stumbled up the stairs and burst onto the brilliantly lit stage. Blinking in disbelief, I heard applause pouring from the packed auditorium. People were standing on their chairs. Even the judges were giving me a standing ovation. I was in shock.

A crown of daisies, roses, and ferns was placed ceremoniously on my head. It was too big and slipped down over my ears. A brass trophy was thrust into my hands, while a white satin banner affirmed that I was indeed being named Miss Vermont of 1956.

My eyes scanned the audience for my parents' faces. Mother was weeping copiously on the left side of the auditorium. Dad and Nora were clapping wildly on the right. For one addicted to pleasing others, it was a heady experience.

Suddenly I felt somehow terribly alone, vulnerable. The thorns in a mountainous bouquet of red roses pricked painfully at my arm. In all that noisy, spotlit room, only the pain seemed real.

Though I didn't know it, the pain had just begun.

4

Into the Fast Lane

Suppose a bottle should materialize before him full and unopened. Once assured of its reality, how calmly then, all excitement gone, he would open it and pour, almost not needing it in the security the sight of it gave him. But he would drink it, of course. He wouldn't care how bad it tasted—un-iced, without water or soda, lukewarm, stinking, throttling. He would drink a good half-glass at once— and at once the pricking nerves would die down, the thumping heart quiet, the fatigue and ease come warmly over him at last. That's what liquor and only liquor could do for him. . . .

—Charles Jackson
The Lost Weekend

THE MORNING AFTER THE VERMONT PAGEANT I AWOKE IN MY FATHER'S home to the scent of roses. I rolled over in bed and touched the gleaming trophy on the nightstand. So it wasn't a dream; it had really happened.

"Here's the morning paper, Miss Vermont," my stepmother chirped, bringing coffee. "Your picture's on the front page."

Indeed it was. There above an expanse of bare shoulders, a mass of greenery and flowers obscured my eyes. Only the tip of my nose protruded out from under the foliage like a shiny cautious mouse.

"Oh, no," I groaned. "I look like a tossed salad."

Weeks later the same horrid picture glared at me from the slick pages of *Confidential* magazine. The magazine staff had amassed the most unflattering photos of state pageant winners they could dig up and concocted what they felt was a real pageant exposé. The caption under my picture: *Is This Vermont's Best?*

Shortly thereafter each contestant received an unsettling flood of letters from members of a fundamentalist group as we prepared to go to Atlantic City for the Miss America Pageant. We were informed through elaborate maps and diagrams that we had chosen the road to death and destruction.

My oversized crown was not the only unflattering aspect of the newspaper picture. At 146 pounds I was twenty pounds overweight. A stint as tennis instructor at a summer camp turned out to be a good way to prepare for the Miss America Pageant looming ahead in September in Atlantic City. The campers monitored every mouthful of food I ate and by late August the twenty pounds were gone.

Meanwhile, filling the duties of Miss Vermont had its perilous aspects. Who, for example, would have anticipated horse shows? At these appearances it was my duty to tromp to the center of the field, present trophies to the victorious riders, and pin the ribbons to the bridles of their snorting, gasping mounts. Since horses have terrified me since early childhood, these ribbon ceremonies represented pure torture.

The Stowe Horse Show was almost canceled by heavy rains. But "the show must go on." At the judge's nod I picked my way gingerly through mucky clods of earth toward the biggest, blackest stallion ever born.

As I approached, this black monster reared up on his hind legs. When his right front hoof came down, it pummeled my left foot into the slime, driving my periwinkle pump several inches into the mud. Only my stocking foot emerged, undamaged—but how does one walk off the field with one shoe? My fear of the beast turning to indignation, I began to dig furiously for the submerged pump. Some unseen force was pulling it in the opposite direction. By now my white gloves were two clunky paws. At last I struggled upright, clutching the oozing shoe, while a nervous judge helped me off the field past the tittering onlookers.

Unaware that my insecurity had turned me into an all-out people-pleaser—especially with men to whom I automatically looked for approval—I accepted blindly all suggestions put forward by the Vermont Development Commission, the Chamber of Commerce, and the Vermont Ski Association. In spite of the fact that September was breaking all heat records, I agreed to travel to Atlantic City dressed in ski garb. The outfit they chose made me look like a raspberry-colored walrus. (Raspberry was the newest and most daring shade in ski wear in 1956.) But I lived to please.

Departure day at Burlington's airport was the initial test. Approaching the plane I had my first tussle with my cumbersome skis and poles. Even though laced together, they clearly had a mind of their own and poked out of my frantic grasp in all directions. Trying to be terribly nonchalant, despite the trickles of perspiration running down my face in the 80° heat, I stumbled up the narrow stairs of the DC-7, my ski boots massive lead weights. Somehow the stewardess and my traveling companion, a charming woman named Barbara who was director of the Vermont Pageant, got me sandwiched into the narrow seat.

Getting off the aircraft at LaGuardia Airport for a change of planes was difficult, but a breeze compared to my encounter with the revolving doors inside the terminal. Barbara sensed impending disaster. "Clasp your skis and poles close to your body," she urged. "Take teensie steps until you get around, then step out slowly."

Holding my breath, I clattered into the swirling cubicle. What happened next I can hardly describe. Skis, poles, and I flew from the spinning contraption like an exploding pinwheel. Barbara darted to safety as a pole zipped by her head. Stunned onlookers peered in disbelief at the tangled mass of steel and bamboo that lay sprawled on the marble airport floor.

We did eventually arrive at the Atlantic City airport where we were whisked into a pageant limousine. When we emerged at the Claridge Hotel, Barbara collared the photographer who had been assigned to record my arrival. Where was that promised brisk breeze from the ocean? I was about to faint from the heat.

"Let's set up the shot on the beach," the photographer suggested, leading us across the boardwalk and onto the scalding sand. There I strapped the skis to my boots and crouched in my best downhill position while he took shot after shot.

The blowing sand caked my perspiring face and stuck in my teeth. My knees felt as though they'd never unbend.

Afterward I clomped off dutifully to Registration. Assembled contestants floated about the palatial ballroom perfectly coiffed and groomed—immaculately pressed, buttoned, and zippered. Over in the corner, by contrast, was propped a wretched raspberry robot, fumbling with skis and poles.

The net result of the ski publicity attempt:

1. No picture in any paper—local or otherwise.
2. Two huge blisters on both heels.

Pageant week continued to provide one glitch after another. I spilled food and broke my zipper at a crucial moment. At the end of my talent presentation I forgot the presence of stage hands and bustled about cleaning up my equipment, causing, to my mortification, a burst of laughter from the audience.

Yet this very laughter served as my escape. As I'd learned, first as a child, then as a teenager, I covered my confusion with pranks and pratfalls. It won me acceptance from the other contestants, who voted me Miss Congeniality.

Once again the press handling did little for my ego. One reporter noted that my listed weight of 146 pounds (recorded before I had dropped the twenty pounds) was the highest of any contestant, and wrote this caption under my picture: *Fattest At Pageant Is Friendliest.*

Nevertheless, my future seemed full of promise. The day after the Miss America Pageant (beautiful Marian McKnight of South Carolina won that year), I was flown to New York and introduced to the Broadway columnist Walter Winchell. Winchell delighted in discovering young talent and creating opportunities for them. Thus began an unusual friendship. Probably because my naïveté intrigued him, he took a fatherly interest in my career.

One night I was escorted by Winchell and Joe DiMaggio to a party for Judy Garland at the Plaza Hotel. The small-town girl from Vermont gazed around the room awestruck at the celebrities from sports and show business. In the glow of the flickering candles and flowing champagne, the world seemed a warm and wonderful place. I became hooked on the celebrity lifestyle.

Hoping to launch me in an entertainment career, Winchell got me breaks on television variety shows. But even his clout could not compensate for the fact that I was a lousy actress.

By now I was going to classes at the Parsons School of Design in New York City, and working part-time at the Vermont Development Commission office in the Radio City Music Hall building. There I met the Operations Manager of Disneyland who offered me a job as an artist doing caricature sketches of tourists. Soon I moved into a Newport Beach, California, beach house with three other girls.

After a two-week apprenticeship under a Disneyland instructor, I was assigned a location at Sleeping Beauty's Castle. My first assignment might have served as a warning of trouble to come. A young mother with three sons signed up to have each child sketched. The first two likenesses flew easily from my pad. Not so the third. The little boy wiggled, slid down from his chair, made faces, stuck out his tongue. The first three tries were disastrous, the fourth barely acceptable.

I was close to tears. What was wrong? Why was my hand shaking? Could it have been because of the beach party that had gone on until two that morning? My roommates seemed to feel fine after these late nights. Why couldn't I stop after one or two drinks the way they did?

In any case, the Disneyland job lasted only for a season. Pepsi Cola, one of the Miss America Pageant sponsors, offered me a position in their public relations department with a good salary and an expense account. I moved back to New York City.

One of my first assignments was to go to Providence, Rhode Island, to help with a fashion show promotion put on by the local Pepsi bottler. While strolling down the familiar streets—it was hard to believe three years had passed since my father's phone call ended my stint at the Rhode Island School of Design—an episode occurred that, once again, should have alerted me to the excessive side of my personality.

Ahead I saw a familiar storefront logo: *Kays of Newport*. As a student, I'd drooled over their gorgeous shoe windows, but could never afford a single pair, even on sale. Today the store windows were swathed in wide paper banners. *Relocation Sale! 50–75% off!!*

Seated inside the store on a plush velvet chair, I smiled nervously at the salesman. "I was thinking of a little evening sandal in silver," I said, trying to sound sophisticated.

Soon he returned balancing six shoeboxes.

"Ooooh," I squealed amid a flurry of fuschia tissue paper, as he slipped a gleaming sandal with rhinestone trim onto my foot.

"I'll take them," I gasped enthusiastically, not wanting to appear gauche and ask the price.

"Would you care for something similar in gold?" he asked.

More boxes, more mountains of tissue. "These lucite sling pumps with rhinestone heels are very new. . . ."

If they were very new, I wanted them. After all, I was expected to be a trend-setter, wasn't I?

Back and forth from the treasure trove behind blue velvet curtains he bounced, arms laden with boxes—black patent pumps, red espadrilles, blue-and-white candy-striped "slings," purple iridescent slippers, navy suede sandals, charcoal gray dinner shoes, yellow flats with flower trim.

"Yes . . . yes . . . yes," I kept saying.

By now the tower of boxes around my chair was obscuring me from the rest of the store. The sales staff were clearly impressed. So were other customers. Who was this extravagant mystery woman? I loved the attention.

An hour later my shopping binge was complete: twenty-two pairs of shoes, five matching handbags. One entire month's salary gone. The purchases would be delivered to my hotel that afternoon.

How was I going to pay my rent? Somehow that didn't matter. I floated back to the hotel in a euphoric trance. From then on, shopping would give me what almost amounted to a chemical high.

Dr. David J. Juroe, writing in his book *Money,* comments on just this kind of reaction: "For those inclined toward buying, compulsive spending sprees keep them on excitable highs, away from being bored or listless about life. What really happens is that the compulsive striving, in this case spending, sustains the constant activity that is needed to distract them from the real inner disturbances."

I was to become very much like the Liza Moran described as follows in "Compulsive Shopping" (April 1986 *Glamour*):

> It is 7:00 p.m. and twenty-eight-year-old Liza Moran is in tears because her boyfriend has just called to cancel their dinner date. This has happened four times in the past month; Liza is afraid the relationship is falling apart. She looks at the clock, realizes the stores are open until 9:00 tonight, and heads out the door.
>
> Several hours later, Liza returns home with a $200 cashmere sweater and a $150 pair of suede boots. She would have bought even

more but she had already used up most of her available credit on an earlier $1000 shopping binge that began after her boyfriend canceled a weekend in the country.

The article went on to describe Liza Moran (not her real name) as a compulsive shopper. When anything goes wrong in her life, she spends money. Liza even uses the language of drug addicts to describe her shopping sprees and their guilty aftermath. "I get high when I catch the first whiff of perfume from the cosmetics counters," she says. "I'm flying the whole time I'm in the stores. The crash comes the next day, when I look at the pricetags on everything I've bought. I tell myself I'll never do it again, but I know I will. The high is worth the letdown."

The pace of my own life speeded up. Early morning plane departures. Cabs, terminals, hotel lobbies. Hands to shake, speeches to make, an endless blur of faces and places. Lonely room service dinners. A drink to blunt the loneliness. Better still, two drinks. . . .

The glamour soon began to wear off as I battled the pinchers and strokers who grabbed at me. At times I felt like a plastic wind-up Barbie doll, at other times like a trained seal: "Throw me a fish and I'll balance a ball on my nose!"

"How many other gals are raking in the dough you're making, doll?" one Pepsi bottler asked.

True. I would be silly to quit such a rewarding job. Yet if people only knew how grim it was to live out of a matched set of turquoise Samsonite. Finally I placed a call to my boss in New York: "Mitch, I can't go another mile. I've been on the road now for five weeks straight. May I take a rest?"

"Sure. Why don't you take a few days in Palm Springs and soak up the sun."

Sitting by the pool of a fancy resort hotel, I let the warm California sun melt away my battle fatigue. I knew I was drinking too much.

Often I'd made promises to myself—one more drink and I'd toddle off to bed. Too often there'd been a rising sun on those words. Time only for a shower, a change of clothes, then it was back to the cola wars.

Reaching for the suntan oil I realized hours had passed. The pool waiter was certainly efficient. I wondered if he'd counted all the drinks he'd served me. It didn't matter if he had. I was an important public relations woman. In the big leagues now.

Weaving slightly toward the thatched snack hut, my toe caught in a chaise lounge leg and down I went onto the pool tarmac. Four waiters in safari uniforms leaped to my rescue. Gently they seated me at a glass table under a tilting purple canvas umbrella. "May I bring you something to eat, miss?" one asked.

My skinned knees burned. "Yes, bring me one of those pineapple things with shrimp . . . and perhaps a vodka martini on the rocks."

After all, it was lunchtime and the guys back in New York would be at the Cub Room starting on their Bloody Marys. It was a ritual I missed. The camaraderie. The comfort of that coterie of bodies pressed together at our end of the bar. The Bloody Marys and the inevitable London broil accompanied by soggy sliced tomatoes and mushy green beans. Nirvana!

Another martini arrived. The whiff of juniper pricked my nostrils as the first bracing jolt of the velvety liquid exploded my taste buds.

Wow, Simpson, you're a fireworks gal! You glitter. You flash. You dance in the sky.

Although for me—at least at first—alcohol acted as a stimulant, it is known to depress the activity of the central nervous system.

Drs. Ray Hodgson and Peter Miller, in *Self-Watching: Addictions, Habits, Compulsions,* describe the effects of alcohol as follows: "In small doses [it] results in a lessening of tension and a feeling of relaxation and lack of inhibition. Increased dosage, however, leads to a progressive loss of control over judgement, skills and emotions, often accompanied by violence and aggression. In large doses alcohol poisons the whole system and may result in coma followed by death. Alcohol also has a long history of inducing a dependence which is notoriously difficult to break."

Traveling with the current Miss America became one of my greatest challenges at Pepsi (I was now the Coordinator of the Miss America/Pepsi Cola Scholarship Foundation). It was my responsibility to see that her public appearance schedule was kept within limits. Not an easy task when the host bottler was paying a thousand dollars a day and wanted her to visit his favorite Aunt Minnie for "just a couple of minutes."

Then there were those harrowing evenings when the new queen was to appear at the same function where Mrs. Alfred Steele (Joan Crawford, wife of the Pepsi Board Chairman) was also to be. As Walter Winchell warned: "Don't invite Miss America (any Miss America) and La Belle Crawford to the same party." When it happened, as it had to, we staffers went into maneuvers not unlike a beachhead invasion, complete with walkie-talkies, to make sure those two stellar females didn't cross paths. Mrs. Steele didn't like to share the spotlight with beautiful younger women.

I used to have the cold sweats hearing in Mrs. Steele's icy voice the words I most feared: "Miss Simmmmmmmsunnnnn!"

Joan Steele was a diminutive dynamo in matching couture creations. Her hat, gloves, handbag, and dress were frequently stitched from the same bolt of fabric; those high-heeled sandals with clear plastic ankle straps were her trademark. The famous crystal blue eyes, flashing under the black slashes of her eyeliner, and the stony set of her crimson, butterfly-shaped lips could transform me into a pillar of salt.

I developed an especially close relationship with Marilyn Van Derbur, Miss America of 1958. One evening after a long, stressful afternoon of appearances, Marilyn, her official pageant traveling companion, and I decided to have dinner sent up to her suite in an Atlanta hotel. We ordered filet mignon, which arrived on a pink linen-skirted room-service table, along with a bouquet of pink sweetheart roses.

"Thank God this day is over!" I gasped as we kicked off our shoes and collapsed into chairs about the table.

"Why don't you do just that?" Marilyn urged.

"Just what?" I asked, trying to blink away the rum punches I had gulped down in the hotel bar before coming up.

"Thank God. Why don't you say grace, Sandy, so we can start on this gorgeous dinner!"

I was nonplused. I didn't know a grace to say. I couldn't remember the last time I'd heard one.

Then she rescued me. "That's okay, Sandy, I'll say it. You've had a rough day."

Softly Marilyn thanked God for his goodness, for his protection, for her responsibilities and privileges as Miss America. I suddenly wished I could talk to God as she just had. How many years had it been since I had gone to Sunday school or church? Five? More like ten.

What I couldn't understand was why I wasn't enjoying my life more. I was meeting glamorous and important people; I had a solid income (although never quite enough to cover my shopping flings) and all the travel and excitement I'd ever dreamed of. Yet I was empty and frustrated and needy and scared. Nothing was filling that void in my chest regardless of what I tried to stuff inside me. It was a hole so empty that the wind seemed to blow through it.

I was twenty-two and alone too much. Drinking by myself more and more. On lonely evenings my mind would travel wistfully the "white-cottage-and-rose-trellis" route. Maybe it was time for me to get out of the fast lane and settle down somewhere.

"[The Cinderella Complex] used to hit girls of sixteen or seventeen," writes Colette Dowling, "preventing them, often, from going to college, hastening them into early marriages. Now it tends to hit women after college—after they've been out in the world a while. When the first thrill of freedom subsides and anxiety rises to take its place, they begin to be tugged by that old yearning for safety: the wish to be saved, The Cinderella Complex."

But where is Prince Charming when you really want to find him?

For me he turned up in a most unlikely place: Billings, Montana. The Pepsi bottler there had arranged for a blind date for me.

"Oh, no," I groaned, recalling disastrous evenings set up for me in other cities.

"But he's Billings' most eligible bachelor!"

"Maybe the most eligible bachelor in the whole Northwest," the Pepsi supplier chimed in.

"And to top it all off, he's a *doctor*!"

Bells went off in my brain. Wedding bells. A doctor. That rose-covered cottage. Security. Prestige. A man to depend on. A man to love me. I had myself walking down the aisle in yards of white Chantilly before I had even met him.

And when I did, he was ruggedly handsome—a tanned, angular face, sandy blond hair, tall, athletic frame.

The evening flew by . . . a blur of cocktails at his apartment, dinner in a dimly lit Chinese restaurant, dancing at the Skyline Club atop the rimrocks that formed the northeast border of the city. My heart was dancing as fast as my feet.

Parked outside my hotel in the wee hours of the morning, Werner leaned an arm on the wheel of his Thunderbird convertible and looked me straight in the eye. "Young lady, I think I want to marry you."

Nine weeks later we were en route to Europe on our honeymoon.

Who is this stranger I married? I thought, waking in a Paris hotel to see a tousled head on the pillow beside me. We knew so little of each other. A flurry of phone calls, flowers, *I love you* letters. So little time together—maybe two weeks total, if that.

I was suddenly frightened. Marriage was such a big step and I was so ill-prepared. Maybe this isn't really happening. Maybe I'll be getting on a plane in a little while, on my way to some Pepsi promotion. But no, I was replacing one treadmill with another.

The honeymoon was a string of riotous days and nights. Afterward Werner stayed on for a radiology conference scheduled months before, while I went on ahead of him to New York.

A week later I met him at the International Arrivals Building at Kennedy Airport with some unexpected news. I felt sure I was pregnant.

His face dropped. So did the ever-present pipe in his mouth.

"All those people in Billings will think we *had* to get married," I wailed as we headed for home.

"That's okay, honey," Werner assured me. "Let 'em talk. You and I have got the world by the tail."

Wrong. I had a tiger by the tail. Its name was alcohol.

The invitations started as soon as we got back to Billings. Who was the beauty queen from the East who had snatched the town's most sought-after unattached male? Many seemed dying to know. Dinner parties, luncheons, summer barbecues—an endless flow of social engagements.

Usually parties were my forte. Not when I was pregnant, I soon learned. Would I ever be able to stop carrying my little bag of soda crackers?

Sitting on the lawn of our lovely new brick home on Rimrock Road during Werner's long days at the hospital, I'd look out at the college campus across the street, wrestling with the feeling of unreality that still swept over me. The collie dog at my side looked up at me with adoring moist brown eyes. Was this really me? The doctor's wife in Billings, Montana?

Nine months after our marriage our son was born. We named him Bradford, after Brad Frapart, the business manager of the Miss America Pageant who'd become a good friend.

Our Brad was adorable, a cuddly bundle. It was almost like playing dolls, only this doll cried and shrieked.

I'd never been around a baby before. Werner assured me that motherhood would come naturally. In his eyes, apparently, mothers were all-capable. Twenty minutes after his son and I got home from the hospital, he headed out the door to go bowling.

Brad was four months old when my doctor told me I was pregnant again.

To help me adjust to this news, Werner took me to Mexico. We left Brad in Billings with Werner's parents—strict, old-world German Swiss who still spoke with heavy accents. I was intimidated by my mother-in-law. She towered over me in every sense—a devout Christian always talking about "the good Lord." I couldn't remember what was so good about him.

"Bring me another Margarita," I said now to the hovering beach waiter.

Brent burst into the world feet first the following April and never stopped running. An active, cheerful, precocious baby, he kept me running, too. I was lifting him from his bath one morning when I caught sight of Brad grinding the contents of a can of coffee into the gold carpeting of the dining room with his little saddle shoe.

"I'm not cut out for this," I moaned as I raced to retrieve the can from Brad's chubby fist.

"I need a drink."

"I deserve a drink."

Brent was four months old when the doctor again had staggering news.

"I'm pregnant again, Polly," I told the woman who was living with us now to help care for the two little boys.

"That's wonderful!" she exclaimed. "Wouldn't you like to lie down and rest?"

Lie down? I wanted to flee—somewhere, anywhere. There was a Junior League meeting that afternoon. Or was it the Medical Auxiliary? An addict to volunteering, I belonged to every organization in town that could keep my mind off the growing silence between Werner and me.

Here is a description from Nancy Friday's bestselling *My Mother/My Self* of the kind of anxiety-ridden, angry, compulsive woman I had become: "The compulsive housekeeper, the lioness of the Anti-Porn Society, the nonstop charity-worker, the overprotective and critical mother who does it all for someone else's good—who can fault these people out loud? . . . Very often, these women are obsessive/compulsives—suffering from forms of behavior that seem to have nothing to do with anger. Unlike depressed people who turn their anger within, against themselves, the obsessive/compulsives express theirs outwardly—but in such an indirect way they never need face their furies at all."

My third pregnancy was the hardest of all. In my sixth month, regularly as clockwork at one in the afternoon, the premature labor pains would begin. Hospitalization was the only way to prevent the baby from being born too early. For six weeks I lay in a room on the maternity ward. And every afternoon at one the familiar pains would begin.

Lisa was a beautiful little girl with dark curls. Six weeks premature, her head was barely larger than a tennis ball. So fragile. So helpless. So in need of dedicated mothering.

With Lisa's birth I'd had three children in less than three years. Lying in bed in the hospital through the weeks of waiting had been a time for reflection. How little of this there'd been in my twenty-five years! I seemed to have careened through life with my motor racing. I couldn't seem to turn it off. *I want . . . I want . . . I want* had fueled it. "Anything worth doing is worth overdoing" seemed to be my motto.

But surely now, as a mother with three children, I could stop scrambling for whatever it was that kept eluding me. Now I would slow down, savor, devote myself to raising my family.

I returned home with my daughter in my arms and high resolve in my heart—and was soon driven as frenetically as ever. I didn't yet apply the word *compulsive* to my behavior.

Nor had I ever considered an observation like that of Stanton Peele, a social psychologist and probably the foremost expert on addictive behavior: "A person will be predisposed to addiction to the extent that he cannot establish a meaningful relationship to his environment as a whole, and thus cannot develop a fully elaborated life. In this case, he will be susceptible to a mindless absorption in something external to himself . . . his susceptibility growing with each new exposure to the addictive object [or experience]."

In fact, there were a succession of habits I seemed powerless to stop. The more I hated myself for them, the more I did them. The chain-smoking that had begun in lonely hotel rooms now launched the day: I couldn't get out of bed until I had a lighted cigarette in my hand. The four-letter words I'd acquired as "one of the boys" popped out increasingly when I least intended them.

What to do about my bulging waistline? I hated the flab and knew I needed to do something about it. Exercise! Jogging! I bought black tights and a leotard for workouts, a warm-up suit, and a pair of running shoes for jogging. At a women's program at the Y, I groaned and moaned through my first session. Agony! Next I donned my running gear and jogged around the wooden running track until cramps forced me to stop.

Day after day the same routine. Exercise, jogging, then I pummeled my fat on the wooden rollers and my hips with the canvas vibrating machine. My body began to revolt. Cramping, nausea, clouded vision. I simply didn't know when to stop.

"Jogging . . . can become addictive in its own right," writes psychotherapist Howard M. Halpern in *How to Break Your Addiction to a Person.* "I have seen people so obsessed with running and so uncomfortable and anxious about missing a planned run that the activity begins to interfere with other important areas of life." (See section on Compulsive Exercising, p. 231.)

Far from cutting down outside activities, however, I continued to volunteer for every civic cause that came along. I'd open my mouth to say no and out would come, "Of course! I'd be glad to."

Where was my backbone? But Polly was so competent with the children, so patient and steady . . . so unlike me. The only part of married life in which I felt confident was entertaining—and a doctor's wife did lots of that.

So the years slipped into a pattern: part-time mothering, full-time socializing. The drinks required to get me into a party mood grew in number. So did the awkward moments, the blackouts, the incidents I simply could not remember.

Like the turkey episode one Thanksgiving. Our guest list had grown to twelve. Preparation the day before had involved marketing, fixing dishes ahead of time, fussing over the table setting, arranging fresh flowers. Before dashing out the door for a luncheon date, I decided to stop at the supermarket and pick up a larger bird on my way home.

Four o'clock already! How I hated to pry myself away from those after-lunch coffee-and-brandies at the Golden Belle to face the teeming hordes at the grocery store.

The turkey department was a free-for-all. People pushing and elbowing one another to extricate the frosty birds from their refrigerated nests. A twenty-five pound frozen turkey isn't the easiest object to maneuver. As I lowered mine into my cart, waves of dizziness and nausea swept through me. Why did I drink so much? I didn't seem to be able to stop anymore. *I'll start cutting down tomorrow,* I promised myself.

Back at home I faced a new problem: Where was I going to thaw the turkey? *The clothes dryer! The perfect place!*

Thanksgiving morning I crawled shakily out of bed to get the turkey into the oven. A bird that size would take many hours. Now where was it? Not in the refrigerator, I quickly discovered. With increasing frenzy I searched the car trunk, bathtub, downstairs shower, outside barbecue, the roof of the tool shed. . . .

How many drinks had I had yesterday?

An attic-to-cellar search aided by all three children failed to unearth the elusive bird. Twelve guests arriving at three o'clock! I was in a panic. While making a last-ditch sweep through the laundry room, I saw hanging limply from the open dryer door a golden yellow tag: *Swift's Butterball.*

A scarier episode occurred many months later after a party at the Yellowstone Country Club. I didn't remember driving home. Around three A.M. I awakened to see lights glaring into the bedroom window.

Struggling to my feet and pushing back the drapes, I observed a peculiar scene in our front yard. There on the lawn sat the white Jeep Wagoneer I had driven alone to the party. (My husband had had to attend a special meeting and had gone in his own car.) The Jeep's headlights on high beam were blazing into my aching eyes. Both doors were wide open, an inside ceiling light illuminated the car's interior.

At first glance it looked like an errant UFO. I stumbled out the front door and through the thick grass to the lighted vehicle. Cautiously I backed the Jeep across the lawn, over the short curb into the street, then into our driveway.

Back in bed I noted gratefully that my husband had not awakened. *You lucked out this time, kiddo. When are you ever going to learn?*

The next morning I dragged myself out of bed, started the coffeepot, then headed out the front door to fetch the morning paper. As I passed by the Jeep, my glance turned into a stare of horror. Red stains covered the splash panels behind the front wheels. Long, ugly reddish streaks were splattered on the white door. The touch of a trembling finger confirmed my worst fears. It was blood.

What had I done? Had I run over someone last night? Had I killed someone? Oh, my God!

Dashing to the mailbox, I yanked the Sunday paper from the metal box with such intensity I skinned my knuckles. Tearing the rubber band from the paper, I searched the front page for a hit-and-run story, forgetting that of course there'd been no time to make today's news.

Nothing there. Frantically I spread the paper on the ground, tearing and flailing at the pages to find the item I didn't want to see. Still nothing. Gathering up the mangled newspaper, I headed back for the kitchen, my heart pounding. My head was splitting from front to back. What had I done?

"Lord God, I will never, ever drink again! Just tell me I haven't killed anyone and I'll go on the wagon for the rest of my life!"

My husband entered the kitchen and eyed the jumbled newspaper. "Did this thing get hit by a bus?" he asked, reaching for the sports section.

I was standing pressed up against the sink, taking short breaths so as not to faint from fear.

"Did you hear that dogfight this morning?" he went on. "I had to go outside and turn the hose on them. The setter across the street got bitten badly; his blood's all over the Jeep."

The relief that flooded through me made my knees buckle. "Gosh, no, I didn't hear a thing."

My vow never to drink again lasted exactly ninety minutes. As I fixed my children's breakfast I decided to treat myself to a Bloody Mary. I had something to celebrate!

These 1985 statistics from the National Council on Alcoholism are certainly nothing to celebrate: There are 18.3 million adult "heavy" drinkers in the U.S. (who consume more than fourteen drinks a week). Of these, 12.1 million are alcoholics (one-third of them women)—an increase of 14.3 percent since 1980.

New research indicates that women apparently metabolize alcohol differently from men—due, perhaps, to hormonal levels; the menstrual cycle; birth control pills; or even to women's lower percentage of water content and higher percentage of body fat.

Whatever the cause, observes *Ms.* magazine (February 1987), it adds up to the fact that "alcoholism and all its health consequences tend to 'telescope'—proceed at a much faster pace within a female body."

Researchers for the *Ms.* survey, moreover, found that as drinking increases, so does other addictive behavior.

Alcohol, drugs, tobacco and food, according to psychoanalyst Theodore Rubin in *Compassion and Self-Hate,* "are often used as sedative and anesthetic devices in an attempt to relieve self-hate. [Such people] put themselves into a temporary haze in order to escape their feelings. . . . This device is also unfortunately and nearly always unconsciously used as a form of slow suicide."

Are You an Alcoholic?

(The Johns Hopkins Questionnaire)

	Yes	No
1. Do you lose time from work due to drinking?	___	___
2. Is drinking making your home life unhappy?	___	___
3. Do you drink because you are shy with other people?	___	___
4. Is drinking affecting your reputation?	___	___
5. Have you ever felt remorse after drinking?	___	___
6. Have you gotten into financial difficulties as a result of drinking?	___	___
7. Do you turn to lower companions and an inferior environment when drinking?	___	___
8. Does your drinking make you careless of your family's welfare?	___	___
9. Has your ambition decreased since drinking?	___	___
10. Do you crave a drink at a definite time daily?	___	___
11. Do you want a drink the next morning?	___	___
12. Does drinking cause you to have difficulty sleeping?	___	___
13. Has your efficiency decreased since drinking?	___	___
14. Is drinking jeopardizing your job?	___	___
15. Do you drink to escape from worries or trouble?	___	___
16. Do you drink alone?	___	___
17. Have you ever had a complete loss of memory as a result of drinking?	___	___
18. Has your physician ever treated you for drinking?	___	___
19. Do you drink to build up your self-confidence?	___	___
20. Have you ever been to a hospital or institution on account of drinking?	___	___

If you answer yes to any one *of the questions, there is a definite warning that you may have a problem with alcohol.*

If you say yes to any two, *chances are you have a problem.*

If you answer yes to three *or more, you definitely have a problem with alcohol.*

5

The Cultist

Real life is harsh. It is constantly injuring our sensibilities. The temptation to escape from it by flight is the stronger the more sensitive we are: We run away in order to protect our sensitivity, to escape the conflict which wounds it. The land of dreams is close at hand, so that one can escape into it at any moment, far from these painful realities. . . . It is a secret treasure into which he pours the best of himself. It is his way of turning the tables on harsh reality.

Paul Tournier, M.D.
The Healing of Persons

*I*DIDN'T WANT TO FACE MY FURIES. I WANTED SOMEONE ELSE TO DO IT FOR me. Compulsive people are particularly vulnerable to the quick fix of mind-bending fads and cults. We are dependency-prone. We want to please. And from childhood I'd been attracted by the invisible world.

"Have you noticed what a vivid imagination Sandra has?" relatives would say of me. Being an only child in a houseful of adults created companionship problems. So I created imaginary playmates. The characters in my fairy tale books became real people to me. Draped in lace curtains and tottering in Mother's high heels, I was Cinderella swirling in the arms of Prince Charming at the ball.

On warm, sunny days I'd scamper through the tall grass of our neighbor's pasture to my magic hideaway in the woods. It was a small mossy shelf to the right of the path, which I pretended was my majestic medieval bed. My headboard was an enormous Vermont maple with low hanging branches, my footboard a bush of wild roses.

Sometimes I'd bring along Ted, my lambskin teddy bear. Ted and I were great friends. I'd prop him up on my chest facing the rosebush, so he could see what I could see. His black silk eyes were far more perceptive than mine and he could spot an elf or a fairy at a hundred yards.

Once as we were sitting there, a yellow butterfly landed delicately on my chest. I hardly dared breathe for fear I'd frighten this glorious visitor. As the butterfly remained balanced there, I felt our souls touching at some mystical level. So real were these fantasies that it was often hard for me to return to everyday life.

Beautiful and innocent childhood fun, surely. Where and how does it begin to turn into something not so pure and good?

We often had a chicken wishbone at our house drying on the windowsill over the kitchen sink. Dad and I would wait till it was completely dried for the ritual of breaking. Whoever got the longer piece would have his wish granted.

Superstition was part and parcel of New England life:

Never walk under a ladder.

If you spill the salt, throw some over your left shoulder.

Never put your hat on the bed.

Never let a black cat cross your path.

Never open an umbrella in the house.

If you leave the house and have to go back for something, sit down and count to ten before proceeding on your way.

There were rabbit's foot keychains and horseshoes nailed over doorways. (Make sure to mount them properly or the luck will slip through.)

Then came a Ouija board craze. Great mysteries were revealed by this means, I was assured by one neighbor. She had special clairvoyant insights and could tell you where you had lost things. The police used to go to her to ask about missing persons. My mind whirled at such powers. In my early teens I made frequent visits to her house seeking answers to all kinds of problems.

Once as a seventh-grader I attended a magic show at the Barre Municipal Auditorium. My friend Betty Lou and I arrived early to get front-row seats. The magician, the Great Garlock, was a character right out of my early fairy tales. Tall and handsome (who wouldn't look that way in a tuxedo—the first I'd ever seen), he wore a magnificent floor-length black satin cape.

He needed twelve people to be hypnotized. Were there any volunteers? Betty Lou and I streaked to the stage. Perched on wooden folding chairs, we stared obediently into his intense blue eyes. "Count backwards with me," he told us. "One hundred . . . ninety-nine . . . ninety-eight. . . ." Somewhere in the eighties I lost consciousness. When I awakened it was to gales of laughter. Later friends told us that after being given hypnotic suggestions, we had scratched frantically as if covered by fleas and shivered violently from icy cold blasts.

Afterward we volunteers stumbled down the steep stairs from the stage. I crumpled uneasily into my seat. Something was wrong. My mind wouldn't focus. I felt confused, disjointed.

The Great Garlock spoke. "If any of you I have just hypnotized have any problems bringing your mind back into focus, I'll be here tomorrow morning in the director's office to help you readjust."

Next morning I made the mile walk back to the auditorium. The building smelled of varnish and perspiration. At my knock the door to the director's office was flung open and there stood the towering black figure from the night before. He was wearing the long satin cape, yet somehow it looked tawdry in the morning light.

"I'm one of the people you hypnotized last night," I told him. "I've felt strange ever since you woke us up. My mind seems fuzzy. Everything's all mixed-up."

"You must be one of the very sensitive ones," the Great Garlock replied. "Really, what I did last night was routine. Perhaps you went into a higher plane of consciousness than the others."

The man in the black cape fixed his eyes on mine and started the countdown from one hundred. I was aware of onions on his breath.

Suddenly I had the strangest sensation—as though something unknown, something dark and disagreeable, were trying to climb right inside me. My heart started pounding. "I don't want to do that again," I wailed.

"But you must if I am going to help you."

"Can't you do it any other way?" I pleaded.

"Well . . . perhaps."

He pulled a chair beside mine and explained that he would call upon a higher power to help me. I didn't understand the words he used after that. *Magicians must have their own language,* I thought.

Ten minutes or more passed. His voice trailed off into a chant. I was feeling very uncomfortable.

"You should have no further problems now, miss," he said at last.

I thanked him weakly and backed out of the room. Did I feel any better? I wasn't sure. A part of me felt violated that had felt safe and secure before that night.

Psychic phenomena, however, continued to fascinate me. It wasn't long after the Miss America Pageant that I visited a woman who told fortunes with a deck of cards.

"Your parents are divorced," she revealed. "They live in close proximity."

Quite true.

"You have just won a national honor," she went on. "It will carry

you into new horizons of job opportunities and influential relationships."

This woman is wonderful, I thought.

The shoe-buying orgy in Providence was my first look at my own
tendency toward excessive behavior. Alarmed by this lack of control
within, I started looking for control outside myself. Soon I was
searching regularly for the "Today's Horoscope" column in news-
papers. If my horoscope said to beware of short trips, I'd hesitate to
cross the street for a cup of coffee.

When marriage to Werner failed to supply the needed external
control, I sought out a psychic in Billings. She called herself
Madame X—a pot-roast of a woman, solid, round, with watery
brown eyes and hair pulled into a tight bun at the back of her neck.
I began to depend on her for most of my decisions.

At one visit (fifteen dollars per session) she announced that we
had been joined by her "spirit guide" who also happened to be her
dead mother. Together they went into the previous lifetimes they
said I'd had, including one as the wife of a cruel Chinese war lord
who sold me as a prostitute. I was anxious to believe these
revelations, my imagination captivated by the intrigue of my
supposed past.

To expand my psychic awareness Madame X encouraged me to
attend the weekly class she taught. At these group sessions, held in
the basement of her modest home, she'd speak of members who
were absent, telling us what they were doing at the precise moment
we were meeting.

One mind exercise she taught was billet reading. We would
write things on pieces of paper, fold them up, and pass them around
in a basket. Picking one at random, we were to feel the vibrations
of the message and "read" it without opening it up. I got to be
pretty good at it.

One of my friends tried to warn me against all this. Influenced no
doubt by her Roman Catholic faith, Lois Ann a stately brunette

with compelling blue eyes, called such practices "occult." They were, she informed me, "an abomination to God." She even brought a Bible to my house one day and read me a passage out of Deuteronomy:

> Let no one be found among you . . . who practices divination or sorcery, interprets omens, engages in witchcraft, or casts spells, or who is a medium or spiritist or who consults the dead. Anyone who does these things is detestable to the Lord. . . .

It struck me as a little far out but I didn't say anything.

The person who brought the most stability into my life at this time was our cleaning woman, Hilda, an outgoing, energetic woman with copper red hair. (Polly had gone to be with her grandchildren.)

Hilda was more than an employee. She was a surrogate grandmother who had great strength, endurance, love, and tenderness. I often turned my responsibilities to my children over to Hilda so that I could focus on civic projects and social engagements.

Sometimes I would catch her looking at me sadly: "Sandy, you've got to spend more time with these kids. They need you. You don't have to volunteer for every committee in town. The years will slip away, the kids will grow up, and you'll have missed the most important time in their lives."

I knew she was right. And I loved my children dearly. But, compulsively driven as I was, I could only overwhelm them with gifts and affection in sporadic efforts to make up for lost time. What little I was able to pass along to them issued right out of my own compulsive traits.

My perfectionism where clothes were concerned, for example. I used my design training to see that the family's wearing apparel was color-coordinated. And one day I discovered that Lisa, age four, was changing her clothes several times a day. If her socks didn't match her dress or sweater, she went into a frenzy, tearing through her dresser drawers for just the right combination. The thought that my daughter was growing up like me was scary.

What I *didn't* give our children was time. My husband and I came home late from a country club party to find Brad, Brent, and Lisa asleep in the hall instead of their bedrooms. For solace—for companionship?—they'd wrapped themselves in their nylon comforters like three little quilted cocoons. Remorse tore at my heart. Why didn't I stay home more? What was I doing to these tender little lives?

Werner, too, was seldom available to them. Every daylight hour he spent at the hospital or tennis court. In addition, his practice took him to other towns in Montana. When I went to Madame X with a litany of complaints against my workaholic doctor husband and his absenteeism, she consulted her spirit guide and reported that we were not right for each other. I already knew that: at the ten-year point of our marriage I was rationalizing my heavy drinking as the result of our deteriorating relationship. Werner and I were two utterly unconnected people wandering in our own worlds. Strangers when we married, the passage of years had not brought us much closer.

What advice did Madame X have for improving my marriage? The psychic shook her head. "You and your husband are working out your karma from other lifetimes. Perhaps the next time around will be better for both of you."

Since I had suffered the trauma of my parents' breakup, divorce was the last thing I wanted for myself and our children. Nevertheless, it took place—legal separation in 1970, divorce the following year. I moved to our weekend home in Red Lodge, sixty-five miles from Billings, and entered the three children in school there.

It was a miserable time for us all. The children missed their father and their friends back in Billings. One fall morning my older son Brad, then ten, announced he was running away. He put on his corduroy jacket over his jeans and shirt, packed a pair of socks, two cans of tomato soup, a knife and fork, and a flashlight in a brown paper bag. Then he headed up the street, kicking the brown and yellow aspen leaves as he went.

I watched him from the living room window, set to jump into the car and follow him the moment he was out of sight. Where the road turned, however, he stopped. For a long while he stood there, head bowed. Then slowly he retraced his steps. Inside the house he emptied the contents of the paper bag onto the foyer floor. "I'm back," he said. I hugged him fiercely, his cowlick tickling my nose.

Brad's unhappiness with the current arrangement remained, however, and a few weeks after this episode he went to live with his father. Several years later Brent would join him.

Meanwhile, I married again. The answer to all my problems, I decided, was another husband. Perhaps this man could fix what was wrong with me, fill that empty place. The need for someone who could show me what to do, who could bring control and order into my life, was compelling.

"Too often," writes Dr. Sonya Friedman in *Men Are Just Desserts,* "women marry to escape their true selves, believing that marriage will make life work for them. Operating under the assumption that they are incomplete, unformed, lacking the capacity to take care of themselves financially or emotionally, they seek out a man who will be caretaker, benefactor, lover, and hero—'everything' to them."

Similarly, psychoanalyst Karen Horney in her classic *Feminine Psychology* referred to "neurotic women who feel unhappy, insecure, and depressed as long as they do not have someone devoted to them, who loves them or somehow cares for them."

My new husband, Randall, was a sharp Billings trial lawyer, a man of striking good looks. The children and I were glad to be back in Billings again, where we could see Brad more often, where Brent and Lisa could visit their father, where I could resume my hectic social schedule. In my obsessive busyness it didn't occur to me that no amount of outside activity, only a transformation inside, could satisfy. In my neediness I continued to cry out for answers from anyone and everyone.

One day I saw an advertisement in the newspaper that read something like this:

> Who Are You? Why Are You Here?
> Looking for Answers?
> Is inner contentment eluding you?
> Come Wednesday night to a lecture of
> *The International Serenity Society**
> and revitalize your life.
> 8 p.m. Comanche Room, Warbonnet Inn.

I have a date with destiny tonight, I told myself as I pulled my car into the overflow parking lot of the hotel. I was disregarding the advice of Lois Ann who had warned, "Sandy, stay away from all that hocus-pocus! You're playing with fire."

I tuned out her words as I hurried up the concrete sidewalk and into the sprawling dark brown stucco building. Inside I found a registration table strewn with alluring color pamphlets of the Serenity Society. I grabbed a handful and headed for the crowded lecture room.

The evening's speaker was a stocky, handsome woman named Velda. She had short salt-and-pepper gray hair curled tightly about a strong square face, and bright dark eyes that snapped knowingly behind thick glasses.

---

* Not the real name.

"The International Serenity Society has totally revolutionized my life," she began. "For years I suffered from depression, asthma, and painful arthritis, but this simple program has given me the tools to overcome these problems. Any one of you can change your lives this way, too."

The lecture lasted an hour. Facts, graphs, humor, even Scripture. Velda had a mixed bag of technical data and psychic techniques. I was captivated by her presentation, wanted to know more, and made a date with her for a special counseling session the following morning.

At 10:45 A.M. I swung into the driveway of the address she'd given me, a crisp twenty-dollar bill in my pocket. Velda greeted me at the screen door and invited me back to a book-lined study. A tall grandfather clock ticked in the shadows reminding me suddenly of Uncle Ralph. Feelings of helplessness, of the desire for some kind of external control, flooded me.

When I was seated Velda explained how she would help me contact my "spiritual guides" through her own guides, a process that involved much eyes-closed concentration.

Apparently sensing uneasiness on my part, Velda assured me, "You have nothing to be afraid of. These guides are spirits who've been with you ever since you were born. Even before that. They are committed to helping you as long as you are on this side."

Further revelation: I had nine guides, which supposedly meant I had a very important earthly mission. Most people have but four or five.

"You are a very old soul," Velda told me, "a master who has returned from many lifetimes. You didn't have to come back this time but *you chose to.*"

My head was spinning, the ticking clock setting the pace of my heartbeat. "What are you trying to tell me?" I asked.

"That you are a prophet," she answered, "with strong visionary capabilities—gifted in intuition, but confused in the feeling part of your psyche."

Before dismissing me, she urged me to attend the summer camp of the International Serenity Society, which would be held in Idaho at a place called Spirit Lake.

Should I go?

How I wished I had Madame X to advise me. She'd died recently of gall bladder trouble—a terribly grubby earthly ailment, I thought, for such an ethereal spirit.

In Madame X's classroom I'd heard about people who received answers via "automatic writing." Back at home I sat down at the kitchen table with pencil and legal pad borrowed from my new husband's desk. With pencil poised, I waited self-consciously for some message from the spirit world. "Should I go to this camp?" I wrote at the top of the page.

Now what? Would some unseen force seize my fingers and spell out the answer? Would the pencil write by itself? How did these discarnate spirits communicate?

For a long time nothing happened. Frustrated, I cried out, "Okay, if there are nine of you guides out there, or in here, or wherever you are, somebody please tell me something."

I felt my arm begin to shake with small tremors. Placing the pencil on the waiting pad, my hand scribbled, "YES. GO."

Thrilled with this outward sign of affirmation, I sent in my application.

I was a cauldron of conflicting thoughts and emotions when I returned from Spirit Lake. Part of my conscious mind was telling me it was all nonsense—maybe even dangerous nonsense, as Lois Ann had warned. Another part was telling me how fascinating this new knowledge was. Why, it even contained Scripture. Well, what sounded like Scripture.

What I didn't realize was that the compulsive woman unrecognized inside me was finding a "high" in these experiences. Psychic phenomena—offering experiences like altered states of consciousness, trances, perceptions of auras surrounding objects, even the exaltation of becoming divine—attract people seeking a mood change, and can deliver just as effectively (and addictively) as alcohol or drugs.

In fact, new research suggests chemical explanations for so-called transcendental states of consciousness ("Anatomy of Ecstasy," *American Health,* January/February 1987). Arnold Mandell, brain chemist and professor of psychiatry at the University of California, San Diego, theorizes that meditation inhibits the action of the neurotransmitter serotonin, ordinarily a brain-quieting hormone. The result: increased electrical discharges. In Dr. Mandell's words, "Affectual and cognitive processes characteristic of religious ecstasy."

Eugene d'Aquili, a psychiatrist and neuroscientist at the University of Pennsylvania, postulates that electrical stimulation of the parietal lobe of the brain corresponds with advancing states of transcendence, all the way to "ultimate mystic experience."

I knew nothing of such chemical explanations, of course, but was drawn by the intrigue and spiritual euphoria promised by the Serenity Society. Since I had agreed to be the Montana representative, our home soon became the destination of a steady stream of visiting ISS "counselors," each one stranger than the last. My new husband, Randall, had welcomed these visitors good-naturedly at first, but his attitude soon changed to frustration, then outrage at the constant intrusions, the endless long-distance phone calls. He was totally turned off by my new psychic vocabulary: chakras, auras, reincarnation, karma.

Desperate for help with my out-of-control drinking and the eating binges with which it alternated, I began calling these counselors for advice. To each I described my inability to concentrate; the mocking, haunting voices in my head; the ugly faces that zoomed in and out of my mind whenever I closed my eyes.

"You've picked up some angry souls from a past life who are out to get you, now that they have your attention," one told me.

"There is an astro-soul counselor in the Denver area," another said. "He could regress you through your former lives to find out just exactly who is harassing you." But the process, it seemed, would take months and be very expensive.

A third adviser suggested I try cold showers. "These dark spirits cannot stand the cold. Cold baths work well, too. You might want to throw in a couple of trays of icecubes." Later this same counselor called back long-distance (charges, of course, were always reversed). "We're having a conference here in Los Angeles this weekend. Friday night at ten o'clock sharp we will all send you our energy. Be standing under a cold shower so you can receive it."

At ten o'clock that Friday night (eleven o'clock my time) I was shivering in the shower stall. Was I receiving the promised energy? The only observable result was a miserable cold.

Days, weeks, months passed while the sinister voices, the hideous faces became more insistent. Nothing could shut them out—not alcohol, not the cakes and other sweets I'd slip into the kitchen to gorge on in the middle of the night.

My weight was now crowding two hundred pounds; coloring and setting my hair, taking time over my clothes—everything had become too much trouble. Once as I was standing in the checkout line at the grocery store, I overheard a woman behind me whisper to someone else, "She was in the Miss America Pageant? She couldn't win a livestock show the way she looks now!"

One day in desperation I remembered that my daughter possessed a two-inch silver crucifix on a black silk cord; I found it in her top bureau drawer and clutched at it for comfort, the sharp edges embedded in my frantic palms. But nothing seemed to help.

Nor any person. My husband was bewildered by the change in my appearance, and my enslavement to the bizarre practices of the Serenity Society. Brent and Lisa would come home from school and greet me with troubled faces. One day when I was out the two of them rifled through my desk drawers and threw out what they could find of my Serenity Society literature, explaining when I discovered the loss that it made me "act funny." I ached to be a real mother to them. Yet I had nothing to give. I was totally consumed with self—self-hatred and self-pity—and spent endless hours in bed with the covers pulled up over my head, the drapes closed to shut out any prying rays of the sun.

I had everything to live for and yet something inside me was pushing me straight into a dark pit.

These days "channeling"—men and women giving up temporary use of their bodies in order to channel the messages of spirits, ostensibly wise old "ascended masters"—has become a multi-million-dollar business. In California, according to the *New York Times* (May 10, 1987), consumers can consult a reincarnated "spirit" for as little as ten dollars or as much as $1,500 an hour. The best-known channels (formerly called mediums) charge admission fees of $200 to $400 at weekend seminars that attract hundreds of people.

The same *Times* article quotes Marcello Truzzi, professor of sociology at Eastern Michigan University who specializes in para-normal research, with this critique: "What we have is a tremendous democratization of religion, allowing many people to be the pathway to the almighty. Everybody has a pipeline, be your own guru; everybody is their own priest. It assuages guilt, tells people that what they are doing is all right. . . ."

Psychiatrist Scott Peck, on the other hand, in *The Road Less*

Traveled, writes tellingly of the attempt to escape the anxiety and pain of being responsible for one's self. It is this anxiety that drives the compulsive person to self-destructive acts and perilous dependencies:

> The difficulty we have in accepting responsibility for our behavior lies in the desire to avoid the pain of the consequences of that behavior. . . . Whenever we seek to avoid the responsibility for our own behavior, we do so by attempting to give that responsibility to some other individual or organization or entity. By this means we then give away our power to that entity. . . . In attempting to avoid the pain of responsibility, millions and even billions daily attempt to escape from freedom.

6

Why Live?

I do not believe a real urgency to die produces the suicidal act, so much as the feeling of not knowing what else to do to ease the Pain. The person is all out of struggles.

—Arthur Janov, Ph.D.
The Primal Scream

IT WAS NOT UNTIL I ATTENDED THE COMPULSIVITY CLINIC, YEARS LATER, that I gained true insight into my suicide attempt. Just as Peggy, in our small group there, had started me thinking systematically about my early years, so another group member helped me look into the depths of the pit I had finally reached.

Ginny was a small, thin brunette with a soft voice, eyes full of hurt, and an apologetic manner. At the Compulsivity Clinic she had listened to the lectures and small-group revelations with no sign of emotion. Confronted by our group leader, Maureen, for her passiveness, Ginny had opened up enough to say she loathed herself and had tried four times to commit suicide.

"You're full of anger, Ginny," Maureen informed her. "That's what's behind your suicide attempts. Suicide, you know, is the ultimate angry gesture."

The mousy little woman shook her head in shocked denial.

"Yes, you are angry, Ginny. You're angry at your father for abusing your mother. You're angry at your mother for putting up with it. And you're angry at them both for neglecting you. You've stuffed these feelings down for years. When they wouldn't stay down, you turned this rage on yourself."

Ginny again denied harboring such emotions.

"Everyone in this room is full of anger at someone or they wouldn't be here," Maureen persisted. "We're going to do something about yours right now."

With that she opened the closet in our small conference room and brought out a hollow plastic bat. Then she instructed the rest of us to make a pile in the center of the room of the cushions we were sitting on.

"Now, Ginny, your father is here, sitting there in the corner watching you. Go ahead and whack these pillows as you talk to him. Let it all pour out. You need to get rid of your rage if you're ever going to be healthy."

Protesting that it was silly, Ginny did it halfheartedly at first. Then something seemed to explode in her. Soon the room was reverberating with her fury. Quiet little Ginny had suddenly become the mouse that roared.

"I hate you, Dad!"

Whack! Splat!

". . . for your filthy, rotten mouth!"

Whack! Blap!

"For getting drunk all the time!"

Whack! Thump!

"For beating Mom all those times when she couldn't fight back!"

Thunk! Whap!

"For leaving us without money for food—and spending it on your creepy friends!"

Whack! Crack!

"For cheating on my mother!"

Whap! Klop!

"I hate you . . . I hate you. . . ."

Whack! Whack! Whack!

Ginny was so into it now that she began kicking the pillows right through the open door into the hall, all the while screaming, "I hate you, you rotten, miserable s.o.b.!"

We were drained just watching her. Ginny returned to the conference room red-eyed but peaceful, spent by her outburst of pent-up emotion.

"That sure felt good," she exclaimed. "Now I need some hugs." Soon she was in my arms holding onto me as if she would never let go, our tears running together.

I could identify with Ginny completely. For I was remembering the time several years before when I too had tried to end my life, and the tremendous store of repressed anger I myself had found. Therapy had helped me discover a lifetime of bottled-up rage—which was, Maureen insisted, the major factor in most suicides. I did not have the kind of traumatic memories Ginny acted out. But I had grown up in an environment that blocked the free expression of negative emotion, an environment that encouraged peace at any price.

There might be another reason for my anger, too. The echoes roused in me at the sight of Ginny's distorted face made me wonder suddenly: Did all of us share an inheritance of fear and rage, roots deep in the human past that I could have unwittingly tapped into when I opened myself to the visitations of "spirit guides"? By the time I arrived at the Compulsivity Clinic I no longer believed the Serenity Society's far-out theories about previous existences. But those rage-twisted faces, those shrieks and curses hounding me asleep and awake, had been real enough. Could I have invited Anger itself into my unconscious?

By the time of my second marriage I had also started seeing a psychiatrist, but we did little but spar with words. Several times I was a patient for a period of weeks on the psych ward of Billings' Deaconess Hospital. These served as brief drying-out times only. Back home each time I resumed my drinking to blot out the voices, the faces, the reality of my failure as a human being. One advantage of alcohol as an escape is that it occupies your mind even when you're sober. All my creativity went into subterfuges to disguise the amount I was consuming.

The Tuesday morning trash collection ritual, for example. The moment I heard the familiar grinding of the garbage truck down the street, I would speed out to the garage where sat our two green plastic trash cans. Stealthily I would lift a white dress box from under a dusty stack of discarded magazines nearby and place it into one of the containers.

A gentle shake of the box satisfied me. The bottles didn't rattle: I'd wrap each one in tissue paper and Scotch tape. Inside six empty Smirnoff bottles lay like silent soldiers, shrouded for burial.

Quickly I would open the garage doors, push the cart containing the bottles out to the street, then run back into the garage and fumble for the "door close" button. Whew! One more time I'd gotten the bottles out of the house before Randall had found them.

Getting rid of the empties had become an increasingly challenging ritual. They were always wrapped carefully so that the garbage men wouldn't see them. Heaven forbid these four faceless men (I never had the nerve to look out the window to see what they actually looked like) should know how much I drank!

An all-out commitment to soap operas was another way I drowned out the painful situation around me. The soaps had become my reality since it was too difficult to face my failure as a mother and wife.

At eleven A.M. sharp I'd be seated in the den waiting for *All My Children* to begin. I'd surround myself with a nest of pillows on the black naugahyde couch, make sure I had a fresh pack of cigarettes and sometimes a sixpack of Pepsi with ice bucket and vodka bottle. The phone came off the hook. I didn't want any interruptions.

As time went by, my repertoire of soaps expanded: *The Young and the Restless, The Days of Our Lives, Search for Tomorrow, The Edge of Night, Another World.*

The characters in the dramas became good friends. I talked about them as though they lived next door. Each tragedy I eagerly identified with, each triumph accepted reluctantly. For my own life was still in a shambles.

Even my grocery list was a problem. Why burden my mind with more decisions than I could cope with? List in hand, I'd drive to the small neighborhood grocery store, wrapping the paper around the steering wheel so as not to lose it. Once things got into my purse, they could be lost forever, and I couldn't risk losing anything as important as this. I had to get dinner. That was one function I still performed. Yet it was becoming increasingly hard to stir and sauté and chop and fry.

Grocery shopping would have been impossible without the woman at the checkout counter. Somehow Shelly seemed to look past my rumpled clothes, the dried vomit in my hair, my confused manner. If she suspected that the boxes of candy and cookies were not for "those hungry kids" but for myself, she said nothing. Sometimes she'd leave her checkout line and help me assemble each item on my list. *She cares about me,* I thought on more than one occasion. *I wonder why.*

One morning as I laced my steaming cup of black coffee with a healthy slug from the vodka bottle, I remembered suddenly that Lisa's sixteenth birthday was the following day. By now Brent had joined Brad at his father's; Lisa still lived with Randall and me.

Visions of a glorious birthday celebration suddenly danced in my head. Lisa, radiant and smiling, her bright-eyed young girlfriends seated about a candlelit table. Great baskets of field flowers everywhere. A spectacular concoction of marzipan, whipped cream, and candied violets ablaze with sixteen candles illuminating the contours of her beautiful face. "Make a wish and blow out your candles," I would urge her gaily. "*All of them,* or your wish won't come true!"

But it was only a vision. There wasn't time to invite guests. And anyway, Lisa's mother was . . . too sick to do it. None of Lisa's wishes were coming true. The smiling sixteen-year-old of my daydream was in reality a fretful, stressed young fawn, blinking shyly as she surveyed her disenchanted forest. Life in her stepfather's home was increasingly tense; my remarriage was already floundering under the strain of my progressing addictions.

Well, if it was too late to ask friends, at least we could have her brothers over—make it a warm and wonderful family celebration! At the grocery store Shelly greeted me courteously and helped me find the things I needed for the birthday dinner. Back in my kitchen, I would have just one beer before starting. Three beers and two hours later, I plodded through the motions of unpacking the groceries.

I must make tomorrow special for Lisa! After all, a sixteenth birthday is very important. I recalled how often as a tiny girl she'd stood by my bed with a bottle of Vicks syrup and a spoon in her little hands when she'd heard me coughing in the night.

Closing my mind to such memories, I tried to focus on the job at hand. The cake. The birthday cake. The cake for my child. The child who is taking care of me. Do something special for her, for God's sake!

I picked up the box of chocolate cake mix. *Add two eggs and one cup water.*

I put the box back on the counter, sat down in the middle of the kitchen floor, and wept. I couldn't cope with a cake mix. It was too hard.

A call to the bakery produced an angel food cake with pink icing.

The next day I muddled through a family birthday dinner that was strained and sad.

But not as sad as the following Mother's Day. On my breakfast plate was a card—*To the Most Wonderful Mother in the World*—with a verse that brought wrenching sobs to my gut. Late that afternoon my husband and I went to visit friends. There were many drinks.

At 11:30 P.M. we returned home. The dining room table had been set lovingly with our best dishes and gold-filled flatware. In the center of the table was a bouquet of hand-picked flowers from our yard arranged in my favorite crystal vase. Loving touches from the loving hands of a girl wanting to please her mother, to honor her mother on her special day.

I lurched woozily past the pan of dried-up barbecue ribs Lisa had tried valiantly to keep warm for the Mother's Day dinner. I lifted the lids from the pots on the cold stove. Rice . . . broccoli . . . carrots. I sampled each pot's wilted contents, wiped my mouth with the back of my hand, and headed for Lisa's bedroom.

She was still awake. She had been crying.

Weakly I tried to apologize. "Lisa, I'm so sorry. . . ." The excuse was threadbare by now.

"Where were you, Mom?" she asked, her voice anguished. "I've been so worried. . . ."

"Please forgive me, honey. It will never happen again." As I bent down to kiss her she turned her face into the pillow.

As the number of alcoholics has increased over the years, a new category of damaged people has emerged. According to statistics[4] there are now from 28 to 34 million children of alcoholics in the United States, of whom seven million are under the age of 18. One out of every eight Americans is the child of an alcoholic. Here are further facts:[5]

Alcoholism runs in families.

Sons of alcoholic fathers are four times more likely to become alcoholics.

Daughters of alcoholic mothers are three times more likely to become alcoholics.

Children of alcoholics are often grandchildren of alcoholics.

Daughters of alcoholics are more likely to marry alcoholics.

Many of us who have contributed to these statistics are trying to rectify the damage done to our children, to rebuild their sense of self-worth, to help them find fulfillment in life. It can happen, but not easily or quickly. Because of their upbringing, Adult Children of Alcoholics (ACOAs) develop the following tendencies:[6]

1. Adult children of alcoholics guess at what normal behavior is.

2. Have difficulty following a project from beginning to end.

3. Lie when it would be just as easy to tell the truth.

4. Judge themselves without mercy.

5. Have difficulty having fun.

6. Take themselves very seriously.

7. Have difficulty with intimate relationships.

8. Overreact to changes over which they have no control.

9. Constantly seek approval and affirmation.

10. Usually feel they are different from other people.

11. Are super-responsible or super-irresponsible.

12. Are extremely loyal even in the face of evidence that the loyalty is undeserved.

13. Are impulsive. They tend to lock themselves into a course of action without giving serious consideration to alternative behaviors or possible consequences. This impulsivity leads to confusion, self-loathing, and loss of control over their environment. In addition, they spend an excessive amount of energy on cleaning up the mess.

I was forcing my children, especially Lisa, into this life of misery. I despised myself. The taunting voices in my head were growing insistent: *Give everyone a break . . . kill yourself. Go ahead! Do it! Get out of this life!*

No question about it—everyone would be better off without me. The angry little men who inhabited my inner world had been pointing this out for some time. Sometimes I'd fondle the handle of Randall's hunting rifle. No, I couldn't possibly shoot myself. Or use a razor.

At the very back of the top shelf of the bedroom closet was my exit visa from the world: a cache of sleeping pills that I'd ferreted away in a fat orange plastic cylinder.

Clutching it in a shaking hand one late April afternoon in 1978, I headed for the cherry cabinet where stood a tall, clear bottle of vodka, almost full.

"You'll soon be where you can't do any more damage," I promised myself as I poured the liquor into a water glass at the kitchen sink. Opening the plastic container, I dumped the pills onto the black formica counter where they rolled about in a riot of color.

The yellow wall phone caught my eye. From far away something said, *Don't do this. Think of your children, your husband, your parents. For God's sake, don't do this. Call someone. Get help.*

No. Death would be a welcome relief. I was dead in so many ways already.

Scooping up the skittering capsules, I stuffed them into my mouth and washed them down with an enormous gulp of the bitter vodka. More pills . . . more vodka . . . till the capsules were gone. Then more vodka to kill the taste of the gelatin coating. Two cups of strong black coffee, half-coffee/half-vodka. I reasoned that the hot coffee would melt the capsules in my stomach faster and speed the whole process.

Outside, the gray Montana sky increased the sense of doom. Anyone glancing up at the brick ranch-style house with the white shutters would see a manicured lawn, majestic blue spruces, a glorious willow tree sweeping the ground. No one would suspect that the figure standing at the kitchen window in a red bathrobe was waiting for death.

My lips started forming words. In a quivering voice I began to sing, "Jesus loves me, this I know, for the Bible tells me so. . . ." How peculiar that I would think of that song at such a time! The happy Sunday school tune of years ago marched persistently through my mind. I could think of nothing else.

I placed my hand on the kitchen counter as if it were a ballet barre and practiced ridiculous leg positions, all the while singing "Jesus Loves Me."

Did everyone revert to childhood at a time like this?

Drowsiness was stealing over me. I had to get into bed before I collapsed. I didn't want Lisa or Randall to find me on the floor. Locking the bedroom door, I turned back the bed covers, lowered myself onto the cool sheets, and pulled up the blankets.

I plumped the pillow around my head, the way Mother used to tuck me into bed at night. My eyes scanned the familiar walls of our bedroom for one final time. On the dresser the chocolate brown digital clock stared back at me, its green fluorescent numbers blipping away the final moments of my life.

My eyes rested on a framed watercolor of a red barn. A Vermont barn. Then inky blackness. A howling wind. Nothingness.

Where was I?

I smelled adhesive tape and ether. A blinding light was shining from somewhere above.

Then the sound of my husband's voice: "Sandra, are you awake?" Randall's anxious face looked down at me.

I struggled to comprehend. The pills, the darkness . . . but I wasn't dead.

"Who found me?" I managed to mumble.

"Lisa," my husband answered. "She crawled through the bedroom window."

Self-loathing filled me. Lisa had found me. I had planned all this carefully so that she'd be spared needless horror. What kind of monster was I?

"You've been in Intensive Care for twenty-four hours," Randall was saying. "It took three medical teams to bring you around. They'd given you up—someone felt a faint heartbeat. You were lucky. . . ."

I didn't feel lucky.

I felt sick. Despairing. I couldn't even succeed at killing myself. I rubbed my nose and my fingers came away stained with dark gray crystals. Charcoal. They had used it to save my life. Why had they bothered?

I had reached the bottom of the pit.

Fully thirty percent of all suicides, according to the Department of Psychiatry at Cornell University, are committed by people suffering from severe depression mixed with alcoholism and drug abuse. Recent statistics on suicide, available through the National Center for Health Statistics, indicate that in 1985 there were 28,620 *successful* attempts at suicide. Many more people than that attempt to kill themselves every year—for a variety of reasons.

"It seems incongruous," writes Arthur Janov in *The Primal Scream,* "to say that the aim of killing oneself is to live, but my experience with the attempted suicides makes it difficult to reach any other conclusion. . . . As a rule, the attempt at death is one more neurotic plea to be loved. In this sense, the attempt at death is a cry for life."

7

Breaking the Cycle

At the time any person comes for psychiatric help he is lacking the most critical factor for fulfilling his needs, a person whom he genuinely cares about and who he feels geniunely cares about him.

—William Glasser, M.D.
Reality Therapy

*I*T WAS AT THE BOTTOM OF THE PIT THAT CHANGE FOR ME BEGAN. I HAVE since come to learn that this is typical of compulsive personalities. So long as we can keep up the slightest pretense of normality, we deny the seriousness of our problem. Nor, until a crisis comes, do those around us confront us with our unacceptable behavior.

With my near-suicide all this changed. At the insistence of my psychiatrist and my husband, I entered Montana's hospital for mental disorders at Warm Springs, two-hundred-fifty miles from home, and one of very few facilities in the state then available to treat people with addictions.

I arrived at the hospital dazed, lethargic. There were perhaps eighteen men and women on the ward where I was placed; addicts at that time were mixed in with the mentally ill. The best way the staff knew to keep their charges functioning and manageable was through medication.

The turning point for me occurred in this hospital, but it did not come through chemicals; it happened in another, totally unexpected way.

As one hopeless day slid into another, I sat staring through the greasy, nicotine-streaked windows at the dazzling blue Montana sky outside. How had I gotten myself into such a miserable state, locked up now like a criminal? I didn't want to answer that question, really. For whom could I blame but myself? Two husbands, my children, my parents, my friends had tried to help me. Lord knows how hard they had tried.

Family visits were infrequent because of the distance. Friends sent me helpful books. One, *Beyond Our Selves* by Catherine Marshall, I carried about for days, but never got beyond the dedication page: "To Len," whoever he was. I seemed to have a block about reading anything religious. At the words *God* or *Jesus* my eyes would simply refuse to focus.

One afternoon my roommate, "Jackie," a wispy, angular waif with sad, dark eyes, and I were sitting on our beds waiting for the dinner bell to ring—a signal for us to line up by the front door to be counted before being picked up by the asthmatic old bus that took us all to the central dining hall. Just then a nurse brought a new patient to the room adjoining ours. The young woman collapsed on her newly assigned bed, sobbing and plucking at the bed covers.

Jackie and I looked at each other uneasily. This show of raw emotion was not uncommon at the hospital, but the moans of this poor girl were unnerving. "Oh, Jesus! Jesus! Jesus!" she intoned over and over.

"Karen, try to pull yourself together," the harried nurse implored. "It's almost dinnertime!"

"I don't want to eat, I want to *die*," came the muffled sobs.

Catching sight of Jackie and me, the nurse came to our doorway. "Karen is very upset. She was to be married next week and her fiancé has been killed in a car wreck. Perhaps you two can speak with her and persuade her to come to dinner with the rest of the unit."

Jackie got up swiftly from her bed and stepped into Karen's room. I shuffled self-consciously behind her, alarmed at this new patient's wailings and writhings. Karen was not to be consoled. "Jesus, help me!" she kept crying out. *"Please,* Jesus—help me!"

I was to hear these words hundreds of times in the days that followed.

When Jackie and I returned to our room after dinner, we were startled to discover Karen up and walking regally about the hall. The change in her appearance was startling. Before she'd been a crumpled, sobbing body in rumpled sweater and jeans. Now her short auburn hair was neatly combed, framing a gracefully beautiful oval face. Huge luminous brown eyes shone beneath thick lashes. She had changed into a long white bathrobe and white slippers, giving her an angelic appearance as she glided down the hospital corridor.

I was struck by her loveliness—such a powerful contrast to the other disheveled, vacant-faced patients. She fascinated me and frightened me. I wanted to reach out to her, but her constant calling on Jesus grated on my nerves.

As a little girl I had loved to hear Aunt Ethel tell us Bible stories and to stare at the picture on the Sunday school wall of Christ holding the lost sheep. Somewhere along the way I had lost that connection to him. So I felt a grain of envy for Karen's faith. Even through the personal torment I sensed within her a quality of grace.

Later that first week after Karen arrived I was alone in the room when I looked up to see her in the doorway. "May I come in and talk to you?" she asked shyly. "I'm scared of this place . . . of some of the men. . . ."

This was the first of endless visits to our room. Karen seemed to appear in a puff of smoke—suddenly she'd just be there. It soon became apparent that Karen had appointed me her special friend and protector. I never had to guess who was behind me in the food line, her beautiful brown eyes searching for assurance that it was okay for her to be around. She'd be waiting in the corridor when I got out of the shower room, by the door at the close of my therapy session.

Before long we became close friends. She shared her love for Jim, her deceased fiance, the dreams and plans they'd made for their lives together.

One sultry July night, tossing restlessly in the heat of the stuffy hospital room, I was aware of Jackie's deep, regular breathing in the bed next to me. How could she sleep in this oven?

Then I sensed another presence in the room. Half-sitting up in my bed, I saw a familiar white-robed figure. There was Karen standing in the doorway, her long robe startlingly bright in the moonlight.

As Karen approached my bed I could hear she was crying. "Oh, Sandy, does Jesus love me? Does Jesus *really* love me?"

The pleading in her voice sounded as though this was the only thing in life that mattered to her.

What to do? What to say? Some instinct in me longed to comfort this weeping child. I got up gingerly, not sure how to console this quivering soul—how to reassure anybody of anything. Taking Karen in my arms, I patted her damp hair. It had been a long time since I'd held anyone to offer comfort. I'd always been the one demanding comfort.

Clearing my throat awkwardly, I said, "Yes, Karen, Jesus loves you."

Her sobbing stopped in an instant.

My heart was beating furiously. I felt cold and warm at the same time.

Karen detached herself from my embrace, wiped her eyes with the back of her hand, thanked me in a voice of childlike gratitude, and slipped back to the adjoining room.

I lay back down, puzzling at a strange lightness, almost giddiness, that was pulsing through me.

The full moon dipped lower in the west. The room seemed filled with a fragrant coolness.

I slept peacefully until dawn.

As I write these words eight years later, I am filled with awe at how a fragile little event like this can change the direction of a life. We compulsives travel down one road after another, willfully driven on toward growing darkness and a dead end. In fact, road signs along the way warn that we proceed at our own risk. But pride and stubbornness compel us on.

Then something happens. Perhaps an encounter with another traveler, the breakthrough of a new idea. A change takes place— perhaps only a slight change, as in my case through Karen, but a change nevertheless. The traveler changes direction, hesitantly at first. And the way becomes lighter.

The turning point for me was no more than a flicker in my spirit. Shortly after her nighttime visit Karen was discharged, her leaving as sudden as her arrival. Lying on my bed one early morning a few days later, my eyes drifted to the room next door, resting on the rumpled bed that had been Karen's. Priscilla, a burned-out rock singer, was now camped there. Her bed was a shambles of posters and *Rock Star* magazines. A hand-tooled leather belt with thunderbolts etched around the word *rock,* hung limply to the floor like a fleeing snake.

A chill rushed over me. I recoiled at the thought of this violation to Karen's special place. She'd brought such light to those dreary surroundings.

Shifting to a sitting position on the side of my bed, I stared out the window into the small grassy courtyard. The morning sun had appeared over the building annex, exposing the drabness of our rooms. The windowpane was covered with dusty rivulets from last night's thunderstorm. How I longed to polish the window to crystal clarity. The dirty windows everywhere represented more walls— transparent walls, but *walls* further reinforcing my feeling of confinement.

Glancing down at my lap, I was astonished to see my hands in a prayer position. Across my skirt and onto the floor marched a shadow pattern from the slotted roof overhang—a pattern of *stripes*.

"By his stripes we are healed."

Where had those words come from? Of course! I'd heard them as a child in Vermont from Aunt Ethel. I didn't have any more idea what they meant now than I had then, except that they were somehow good words. Strong words.

My eyes went back to Priscilla's snake belt on what to me was Karen's bed. What if there really were two worlds at war, good and evil?

The breakfast bell jarred me back to the reality of hunger pangs. I really felt hungry! I hadn't felt anything for so long.

"Good morning, Gus," I chirped to our pudgy Scottish bus driver.

"Well, gud mawrnin' to you, Miss Sandy. An' if you aren't a bright-lookin' lass!"

After breakfast, another change. Somehow this morning the thought of gulping down my nine o'clock medication was repellent. The inevitable line was forming, patients clutching yellow Dixie cups to receive their juice and pills.

I inched forward at the end of the "meds" line, my eyes sweeping the dingy lounge strewn with old magazines and pots of pathetic scrawny plants, finally resting on the blaring TV set suspended from the ceiling (a precaution to keep the inmates from wrecking it). I saw NBC announcer John Chancellor appear:

"We interrupt this program to bring you a special news bulletin. The Pope has died in Rome." I felt a rise of tears burn my eyes. Why should I react? I wasn't even Catholic. I remembered with a pang the off-color stories I'd told about the Pope. Being funny had given me power. All at once I was repulsed by my "gutter humor" which, like foul language, slipped so readily from my tongue.

I had almost reached the cart where two nurses were mechanically filling the cups and dispensing the medications. I didn't want to swallow these pills anymore. What would happen if I didn't take them?

As the person in front of me moved away, I approached the nurses' station with newfound resolve. "Here are your meds, Sandy." One nurse filled my Dixie cup while the other proffered gray capsules in a small pleated cup.

Her tired blue eyes stared at me as I popped the pills into my mouth and swished them quickly under my tongue, at the same time swallowing the canned orange juice "chaser."

As they pushed their squeaky cart back to the nursing station, I slipped into the women's bathroom. My heart was pounding as I entered the wooden stall. Flushing the toilet, I spit the bitter pills into the swirling water.

No more pills. The words seemed to come from outside of myself. Suddenly it mattered what I took into my body.

"Going against medical advice can be dangerous," my first husband had said many times from hard-won experience as a doctor. True, if arbitrarily you discontinued medication for something like diabetes. But these pills were chiefly to pacify and control.

Leaning against the rough plaster wall, I felt a tremulous stirring of well-being in that squalid little stall.

Like many women alcoholics, I had become addicted to prescription drugs, creating a dependency I was hardly aware of. The addiction continued when I was institutionalized during the 1970s because the use of drugs was a standard procedure in the treatment of patients during this period. Today most treatment centers have patients go through a detoxification procedure before entering their program; drugs then administered are done only after careful evaluation of the patient's medical history.

Many of these treatment programs, moreover, see a good rate of success. Kitty Dukakis, for example, wife of the Massachusetts governor, announced in July 1987 that she had been treated successfully for a secret twenty-six-year addiction to amphetamines—diet pills. "I am now drug-free and I have been for five years," she was quoted telling an audience. "I'm very proud of that. . . . I am telling my story because I want to help others."

It was a sign of the times that her confession elicited not criticism but respect, and even sympathetic identification.

As knowledge has increased about cross-addiction (for example, a patient is freed from an addiction to alcohol only to become addicted to sweets), patients are treated for their basic compulsive-addictive personality disorder. Cross-addiction, for me, also meant that at one time I was addicted to several substances (alcohol, tobacco, sweets, etc.)

At the well-publicized Betty Ford Center in Rancho Mirage, California, only ten to fifteen percent require prior hospitalized detoxification, but it takes at least a week for the different drugs to leave a patient's system. Whether the problem being treated is alcoholism (their number-one problem), cocaine or prescription drug abuse, or often a combined addiction, that first week represents the hell of withdrawal—shakes, headaches, nausea, and exhaustion.

Even withdrawal, however, is only the first step. The person trying to break any addictive pattern is subject to an extraordinary degree of internal conflict. She wants to break the pattern and she doesn't want to. Symptomatic of this conflict: *dissociation,* a sense of separation from oneself, which sometimes results in a woman's feeling like a helpless spectator to her own self-indulgence.

"Dissociated feelings," write Drs. Hodgson and Miller in *Self-Watching,* "are linked with anxious and depressed states of mind in which willpower, planning, and reasoning are difficult to sustain. In helping people to overcome habits, then, it is not enough to identify why habits arise and how they are triggered. The individual must be equipped with the necessary skills to survive episodes of conflict, when morale and motivation are likely to be at their lowest ebb."

8

Do It Now

*To acknowledge {our necessary losses} and nevertheless find
our freedom, make our choices, recognize what we are and
what we might be, is what a responsible adult is all about.
Bowing to necessity, we must choose. This freedom to choose
is the burden and the gift that we receive when we leave
childhood, the burden and the gift that we take with us
when we come to childhood's end.*

—Judith Viorst
Necessary Losses

WHAT WAS THIS CHANGE INSIDE ME AFTER KAREN?

At first it was simply in my attitude. Less despair. A glimmer of hope. And the resolve to take no more of the daily medication.

When there was heavy traffic in the john, I would slip the pills into an empty cigarette pack and hide them temporarily in my suitcase. I was careful about this because I'd seen what happened to patients who refused to take their medication. Off to the "Quiet Room" to be strapped to a table and given their medication by injection.

I couldn't risk discovery. My progress was slow—imperceptible some days—but I rejoiced at the new freedom I felt. Freedom from the inner fuzziness produced by the Quaaludes and the effect of the Thorazine, which seemed to fling my nerves against my body walls while I drifted in and out of reality. How could I ever get well in a psychedelic haze?

I knew that for some patients—the more violent—chemical stabilizers were the welcome alternative to physical restraint. Yet I sensed that in my case true recovery could not begin until I was free of artificial aids.

A second resolve was to regain my sense of personal dignity. My clothes had been confiscated for "special laundering" when I was admitted. There had been a forced shower and shampoo ordered by the impersonal admitting physician who inspected me like a side of beef, charting my scars, birthmarks, and tooth fillings. Even my wedding ring was taken from me, the last vestige of my "belonging" to somebody.

I felt like a faceless number among murderers, rapists, manic-depressives. Every conceivable type of mental illness was baking in an asphalt pressure-cooker. Helplessness and despair had all but swallowed me whole.

To restore my sense of dignity, I began spending more time on personal grooming, taking more interest in my crafts class, even standing straighter. I stuck all my greeting cards on the wall over my bed as a cheery reminder that I was loved.

As I lay on my bed during rest time one afternoon, my spirit felt lighter. I fell asleep contemplating a return home to my family. Then a nurse was shaking my shoulder. "Wake up, Sandy. The staff wants to see you at once."

I followed her apprehensively down the corridor. What could the staff want to see me for?

As I entered the conference room I saw nurses and doctors assembling in a circle of chairs ready for "report." They were sipping coffee, shuffling papers and patients' charts. My eyes fell on Harry, the hospital administrator, the ever-present unlit cigar jammed into the corner of his mouth. Today he looked particularly disgruntled. My heart sank. I was in trouble, but I wasn't sure why.

At a nod from the nurse I threaded my way past the outstretched feet and lowered myself into an orange plastic chair.

"It has been brought to our attention that you have not been taking your medications," Harry began. "Unswallowed capsules were discovered in your suitcase this morning. Not taking your prescribed medicine is a serious violation of hospital rules. Do you have anything to say for yourself?"

Panic gripped me. Visions of being strapped down in the Quiet Room almost paralyzed my voice. Then something happened. My voice acquired strength. Purpose. I requested formally to be taken off all medication. To my surprise I had moved suddenly from defense to offense.

"I also need a week at home with my family to see if I can adjust to the outside world. Please," I concluded, "just give me a chance."

Surprised looks. Clearly they had been caught off-guard.

"Reactions?" Harry queried his staff.

At first there was mild dissent. I pressed my point, stressing the progress I had made in recent weeks.

"I'll need to clear it with your doctor," Harry said uncertainly. "If she says you may go, I guess there's no reason a week at home wouldn't be all right. Okay, staff?"

There were reluctant nods of agreement around the circle. When queried, my doctor, a warm-hearted Filipino woman, was favorable. The only stipulation: stay on my medication. Before week's end I was on a bus to Billings.

My husband was waiting at the bus station. On the drive home our conversation was strained. Later I stood in my own kitchen for the first time in four months and looked about in childlike wonder. Was this really my home? Somehow everything looked strange. Different.

I was suddenly aware of the depth of my emotional and physical exhaustion. As tired as I was, however, I dreaded going to bed with this stranger I was married to. Randall must have felt it, too. A silent wall separated us that night. He, so vibrant, bright and productive; I, so frightened and uncertain, a failure at everything.

The temptation to stay in bed the next morning was nearly overwhelming. A late August breeze was puffing the green shantung drapes in languid little bursts. Why not just roll over and go back to sleep? It would be so easy to do that. I really wanted to.

Yet deep within a kind of inner knowing gnawed at my soul. If I didn't get started right this morning, my life might never get straightened out. Today was the first day of the rest of my life. With this realization came the practical message I most needed to hear: *Get up! Get moving! Do something to help yourself! Do it now.*

There had been countless mornings when I'd had this choice and had chosen to avoid the world, to hide in my bed, blankets pulled over my head. When I finally would get up, I would go from doctor to doctor, psychic to psychic, friend to friend, desperately hoping one of them could "fix" me, somehow transform me magically into a whole person, sound of body and mind. The answer over the years had become agonizingly obvious: no one else could do it for me. The effort to change, to get well, was going to have to start with me.

In describing this freedom to choose, Dr. Theodore Rubin in *The Winner's Notebook* writes: "The decision I arrive at is uniquely my own and born of my freedom to struggle through my feelings to either act or not act. . . . This kind of freedom to feel and to decide and if necessary, to experience conflict and to struggle through conflict to an answer, produces values. This kind of tapping of one's own feelings and arriving at one's own individual values produces a sense of self-responsibility and identity."

Now, from my bed, I gave myself a set of commands: "Get up, take a shower and get dressed!" My body obeyed reluctantly. These seemingly normal routines had been almost impossible during my periods of depression.

Wiping the steam from the bathroom mirror with the sleeve of my pink cotton robe, I peered at the anxious face that stared back at me. My appraisal:

Eyes: Apprehensive. Needed the usual help from a mascara wand and eyeliner. I hadn't bothered with eye makeup for months.

Eyebrows: A jungle growth. Get out the tweezers fast!

Skin: Ghastly! So dry. Like an alligator suitcase. Alcohol and cigarettes do a job on skin. I looked at broken spider-web veins around my nose. Quick, where's the face cream and liquid foundation?

Hair: A disaster area. Stubborn wisps of gray hair were spiraling through the tangled auburn mop like errant bits of barbed wire. It had been months since I'd cared about coloring my hair.

To signal the change that I hoped was taking place inside, I'd start today to make over the outside. I dressed carefully, then went across the hall to the den where I had a small desk. There I made a list of the things I wanted to accomplish that day. Simple things. Make a date at the hairdresser. Take my soiled dress and slacks to the cleaners. Buy nail polish. I came up with nine items.

As I searched for the hairdresser's number, the old temptations flooded back. *What's the hurry? You've been four months in a grubby hospital. Sit down and have a cigarette. Bet there's a cold beer in the refrigerator. You deserve a break. What are you trying to do—win a medal?*

For a moment it was an all-out battle. My new resolve vs. the old pattern. Oh, how I was tempted.

Do it now!

Those three words snapped me out of it. I found the number and reached for the telephone.

That nagging little voice pursued me all day. *Are you some kind of slavedriver? Take it easy.*

Then from inside the rebuttal: *You've had enough rest. Get on with your life. Do it now.* At the end of the day, to my astonishment, I'd completed all nine items on my list. I'd also made a decision *not* to take the tranquilizers given me by the hospital.

The high point came when I went to get my hair done. What is there about the sounds and smells of a beauty shop that rejuvenate even before the work begins? As Rod, my favorite hairdresser, snipped and whirled me about in the dance that hairdressers do, visions of a new me spun through my brain. For some reason my mind flashed back twenty-two years to the summer of 1956 before the Miss America Pageant. I had felt the same sense of adventure, of a life-changing journey. The clinging coat of depression was dropping away from me like hunks of hair from Rod's scissors.

Wow, what a difference, I thought when Rod finished. I couldn't believe my eyes. The "before" and "after" was staggering.

My husband did a double-take when he walked through the door that evening. "Can this be the same woman I said good-bye to this morning?" he asked with an astonished smile.

Settling for the week into a household routine after months of hospitalization, however, wasn't as simple as I'd thought. The second morning I wondered—should I dust? Should I iron? Should I bake something? Such mini-decisions seemed overwhelming.

I wandered from room to room trying to reacquaint myself with my surroundings. Gingerly I examined each object in the living room as though reintroducing myself to old friends. Why did everything look so strange? A sudden fear began to strip away the fragile self-confidence built up by the first day's small achievements. Would I be able to stick out the week?

Our house was full of old ghosts. Dreadful, painful memories. The chair where I did my heaviest drinking and planned my suicide seemed to menace me each time I passed it. Maybe it should be stored in the basement where I couldn't see it. No, that would be ridiculous. All the furnishings held memories of some sort.

Taking a deep breath, I entered Lisa's now-vacant room. She had moved to her father's house to live with him and her brothers during my hospitalization. I was grateful that the children had pulled together while their mother was falling apart. I wondered if they knew how much I loved them, how guilty I felt.

As my sickness had worsened it had become increasingly difficult to hug them, to show them warmth. My heart had become an icy lump sprouting from stainless steel ribs, my body home to miles of nerves that twisted and tangled around wooden bones. I had felt no life, just desperation.

Lisa's room still had her fragrance about it. The "Love" cosmetics popular with teenagers sat in a pristine row on a mirrored tray. Her dressing table was immaculate, each item in meticulous order. The stuffed animals she'd left behind stared up at me from her red plaid bedspread. Clutching an armful of them, I sobbed into their soft plush bodies. Lisa had often held them for comfort. "Oh, Lisa, what have I done to you? To all of us?"

In the hallway outside her room, the white stucco walls seemed to close in on me. Then they expanded like rubber bands stretching to some far-off horizon. Back and forth. Back and forth.

Perhaps I belonged back in the hospital. Apparently I wasn't as strong as I'd thought. It had seemed so easy in my daydreams at the institution. Was I becoming a robot like so many of the patients there? Had I developed an institutional mentality? Was I unable to make any decisions or do anything for myself?

An insistent inner voice shouted, *No! Get busy. Do something. Do it now!*

This was going to be the toughest battle of my life.

One night that week my husband took me out to dinner. He seemed so proud of the "new me" and scrambled to open the car door and help me with my chair at our favorite table at the Rex Hotel. For the first time in months, I felt special.

As I took dainty sips from my chilled glass of white chablis, I forgot the panic in the hallway. My husband was newly attentive, my self-confidence straining to break through the years of self-loathing. The rather attractive woman reflected in the bar mirror was really me. I tried not to stare at her.

From our table in the back room next to the wall, Randall liked to watch the stream of diners drift in and out. He had the lawyer's observing mind—every detail, every nuance. I admired him so. Yet our marriage had stretched on the brink of disaster for five years. It would take a miracle to breathe new life into it after so much damage.

I tried not to think back to only two years before when we'd sat at the same table on my fortieth birthday. I was on medication and had sat in this same chair in a fuzzy haze. My size eighteen dress did not cover the bulges from my binge eating. I'd felt like an overstuffed chair. A black-and-white print chair. The dress was hideous, but it was the only one I could still get into.

Now, while Randall ordered dinner, I took another sip of chablis to wipe out the memory. A little wine never hurt anyone. After all the heartbreak, I had still not faced up to my drinking problem. . . .

On the six-hour bus ride back to the hospital, I thought back over the ups and downs of the week just ended. The visits with my children had been too short and tense to be satisfying. They had stared at this "new" mother, doubtless wondering whether they dared trust the changes they saw.

What had been accomplished by these seven days? A start . . . and the latching hold of a three-word principle: *Do it now.*

When I arrived back at the Warm Springs Hospital, it was afternoon. Since the entrance door was always locked, I rang the buzzer for admittance. A nurse named Gretchen peered through glass at me. "May I help you?"

"Gretchen, it's me! Sandy. Don't you recognize me?"

"Good heavens, no! You look so . . . good. In fact, you look terrific! Come on in."

Patients and staff alike gathered in the smoky lounge foyer to survey the returning patient. Incredulous stares greeted me, as though I were an alien from outer space.

Harry almost bit through his cigar as he rounded the corner of the nurses' station. "Looks like Billings agreed with you, Sandy. We're about to staff. We'll want a report on your week."

My doctor's round face was wreathed in smiles as she spotted me. "You look wonderful," she declared in her thick Filipino accent. And to the rest of the staff: "We can all see the positive results of home visits!"

Harry was staring at me with questioning, "show-me" eyes. "Give us a report, Sandy."

The pressure was on, every eye in the room riveted on me.

"I-I got along fine," I began. "The hardest part was to walk back into a house that held so many memories of pain and failure—and to know my time there was an experiment only. Could I change old habits? Could I start over? In many ways I was like a baby who had to learn to crawl before she could walk.

"I knew I had to set a schedule for myself that I could follow. I've always put unrealistic goals on myself. I've been such a perfectionist. If I couldn't do something perfectly, I wouldn't try at all. That's been a real trap for me all my life.

"I decided to choose a few simple tasks and do them. Not to expect perfection, but to make progress—any progress—on functioning normally. I wasn't sure that I could, but I did do what I set out to do. I was able to relate to my husband and my children as an adult instead of a sick-o. They were all surprised about that. I got up each morning and showered and dressed and accomplished my housework.

"The first morning I decided to do something about the way I looked on the *outside,* to show that things were changing on the *inside.* I made an appointment to have my hair cut and colored. After coming out of a mental hospital, it took courage to walk back into that shop and face all those beauty operators I'd known so well. I was amazed at the warm way they all welcomed me! Since I'd let fear paralyze me for so long, it felt good to take a risk and have it work out. It's given me confidence to face the next hurdle."

Harry's bulldog face was set in rapt attention. The cigar was teetering in the corner of his mouth.

Gretchen seemed puzzled. "You make it sound so easy, Sandy. It's hard for me to believe you could adjust so quickly. You didn't show that kind of initiative here. . . ."

My heart sank. Did the rest of the staff feel this way, too?

"Let's let Sandy continue," urged my doctor. "I'm sure she has a lot more to tell us."

Now what? What could I add? Frantically my mind raced ahead trying to second-guess what would impress these staffers. I had never been in a situation like it—except the judges' interview at the Miss America Pageant. The thought of that experience in this setting was so ludicrous I almost laughed. It was the comic relief I needed.

"I don't know what else to say," I told them. "Obviously Gretchen finds my new resolve hard to believe. But I've had a lot of time to think while I've been a patient here. What do I want to do with the rest of my life? I want to get well. I want to have a good marriage and be a good mother. I want to be the best I can. Thus far I've been pretty much of a goof-off. I want to get on with the rest of my life."

"All good intentions," Harry interjected. "How do you plan to accomplish all this, Sandy?"

My heart was beating like a threshing machine. My eyes were stinging. What to say?

"I've made some progress. My husband is supportive and my children are anxious to have their mother back. That's a good start. I have a solid base to go home to. I'd like to find a job. I feel optimistic about my life in Billings . . . about my chances to get well there. Frankly, I don't believe I belong in this hospital or any hospital."

My doctor was smiling at me. Patting my clammy hand, she spoke softly. "Staff, I'm going to ask Sandy to leave the room while we process this. Just have a seat in the lounge, if you will."

I struggled to my feet and all but fled.

"Somebody give me a cigarette," I commanded in the lounge area. My roommate, Jackie, offered me an unfiltered one. The bitter jolt of raw nicotine almost spun me around.

"How can you smoke these things?" I gasped.

"I've always said if you're going to smoke, smoke a real cigarette," Jackie retorted. If she only knew how many nights I'd been awakened by her racking cough. Suddenly I felt very tender toward her.

It seemed like hours but it was probably only twenty minutes before I was readmitted to the conference room. Taking the vacant orange chair, I awaited the verdict with lowered eyes.

"It is the consensus of the staff," my doctor announced, "that you are capable of being released from this institution as soon as we can process your papers. We feel you have shown favorable initiative and sufficient resolve to adhere to a solid program of recovery. You've been a cooperative patient. I especially will miss you, and I wish you much good luck in your life outside this hospital."

Tears welled up in my eyes and slid down my cheeks as the staff applauded.

9

The Pain in Change

It is indeed possible for us to mature out of a belief in God. What I would now like to suggest is that it is also possible to mature into a belief in God. A skeptical atheism or agnosticism is not necessarily the highest state of understanding at which human beings can arrive. To the contrary, there is reason to believe that behind spurious notions and false concepts of God there lies a reality that is God.

—M. Scott Peck, M.D.
The Road Less Traveled

*M*Y HOSPITALIZATION AND RECOVERY PERIOD INTRODUCED ME TO A new word in the treatment of compulsive behavior: *enabler*. An enabler is the addict's spouse/parent/child who because of embarrassment or a sense of guilt attempts a cover-up to protect the family, *enabling* the addict to continue his destructive behavior.

An enabling wife is one who calls her husband's office on Monday morning and tells his boss that her hung-over spouse has the flu. A whole pattern of deceptive practices, involving all members of the family, is under way. The addict's sickness is all too obvious; the rest of the family's "sickness" is not so recognizable, yet it is just as real and needs to be treated.

"No matter what personality type you live with," writes Mary Ellen Pinkham in *How to Stop the One You Love from Drinking*, "*all* members of the family will react to the alcoholism, and as the alcoholic becomes more involved with his drinking, *you* become more involved with *him*. You will eventually experience identifiable and pathological behavior that is as predictable as the pattern of the alcoholism itself."

If, as the National Council on Alcoholism estimated in 1985, each of the 12.1 million alcoholics in the U.S. directly affects four other people, then there are at least sixty million people intimately involved with alcoholism.

Family members, through embarrassment and guilt, will try to cover up the destructive behavior of the addict. Husband and children will adjust their daily routines and even go through psychological change in their efforts to protect the addictive wife and mother. In doing this, they became enablers. They not only do not help the addict; they become sick, too. (Check your own co-dependence on p. 262.)

The addict's sickness is usually obvious to family and close friends; the rest of the family's "sickness' is not so recognizable, yet it exists and needs to be treated.

An enabling husband will often assume the role of peacemaker in the family when his wife is an addict. A family friend in his forties, for example, was married to an alcoholic for twelve years. When she died, he took his two young children quickly into a second marriage with a widowed woman and her teenage daughter. The result: tension and conflict in the home.

"When I tried to resolve these squabbles, they dubbed me "peacemaker,' " the friend revealed. "The term was often used contemptuously. It took an Al-Anon meeting to make me see that in my first marriage my role as enabler had, in a sense, made me sick too. My ability to act openly and forthrightly was impaired. I did seek peace at any price and my second family was calling me on it."

My own past is most painful to reflect on, when I see the effect of my compulsive behavior on my family. All tried valiantly to help me: my parents, two husbands, my children, my parents-in-law. All became enablers in one way or another in their efforts to protect me, doing damage in the process to themselves.

My husband Randall, for example, used to watch the liquor cabinet to see how much I consumed. I knew this, so one winter morning I conspired to outwit him. After he left for work I plucked a full bottle of vodka from the cabinet, plotting to use just one shot in my morning coffee. I planned to add a touch of water to fill it up, then restick the seal with glue. He'd never know. Besides, Randall never drank vodka in the winter anyway—just Scotch.

At 11:30 I was on my second pot of coffee and the bottle was half-gone. *I'll run out later this afternoon and get another bottle,* I promised myself. By four o'clock it was snowing and I was in no condition to drive anywhere. I had to sober up and fix dinner. When Randall arrived home at 6:30 the vodka bottle, filled with water, was back in the liquor cabinet, paper seal in place.

Randall sat down in his favorite chair and started to peruse the evening paper. "How about fixing me a vodka and tonic tonight?" he asked.

My heart pounded. I'd gotten caught. "There's no vodka," I murmured.

"What do you mean no vodka? There's a full bottle in there."

"I'm afraid it's full of water."

His eyes never left the paper. His tone of voice never changed. "Okay, then fix me a Scotch and water."

No confrontation. He had resigned himself to the hopelessness of the situation. I wondered how he could go through this little drama without blinking an eye. *No wonder he's such a good trial lawyer,* I thought to myself.

Like millions of other husbands with alcoholic wives, there were times when he did get angry at my heavy drinking, railed at the family upsets that resulted. But over the years he drifted into the role of enabler, protecting me as best he could from myself.

When I returned home from the Warm Springs hospital in the fall of 1978, I had made only the tiniest start on the road to recovery. At my departure my doctor had given me a list of medications to take, most of which I had already decided against using. As the months passed, I had no idea what further steps to take.

There had been some kind of spiritual change inside me, but I didn't know what to do about that either. I even sensed God had spared me—but why? I was still tormented at times by angry inner voices.

My deepest desire was to rebuild my home situation, become a good wife, and develop closer relationships with my children. But how to do that? Probably by working to conquer my destructive behavior patterns. Three areas especially concerned me: smoking, overeating (especially sweets), and drinking. (I was not ready to admit I could not drink at all.) How should I attack these problems? Willpower, I concluded.

A flutter of resolve stirred within me. I wanted to change. I knew I had to change. But how does change happen?

I decided to begin with nicotine, which had already been demonstrated scientifically to engender genuine drug addiction, not just an addiction to the activity of smoking (Edward Brecher, Consumers Union, 1972).

I'd first tried to quit eight years earlier, when a doctor warned me that smoking was damaging my lungs. I'd agreed. It was time to stop. Besides, I hated the spidery lines that were forming around my lips from my constant puffing.

I'd done it back then on sheer willpower. My first act of a morning had been to *not* light up as soon as my eyes opened, but reach for a Life-Saver. If I'd forgotten to leave these "saviour" packs by the bed, I'd fly into a frenzy. What to stick into my mouth?

Ballpoint pens, frayed toothpicks, paper clips, anything I could lay my hands on. Every pair of eyeglasses I owned soon had their bows chewed so badly that they scratched my temples.

What had happened then should have alerted me to the fact that it was not tobacco I was battling—or alcohol, or overspending, or any of my other excesses—but a compulsive personality beneath all the specific cravings. Eliminating cigarettes eight years before had simply brought about a switch in compulsions. Chocolate had then become my slavemaster. In any form. At any time. I'd stir from my bed at ungodly hours and bake a pan of brownies or struggle through the ritual of a devil's food cake mix. "Aptly named," I'd sigh as I stumbled around my kitchen in the darkness.

My clothes had gotten tighter and tighter, as the fibers strained to cover my ever-increasing thighs and derriere. My nocturnal baking sessions baffled my children at first, but soon they looked forward to fresh-baked "surprises" for breakfast. Brownies and cereal. Brownies and eggs. Brownies and pancakes.

After two years off tobacco, one day for no reason I had picked up a pack of cigarettes. "I merit a Merit!" I joked weakly to my drinking companions. The first puff slammed against my throat in a burst of welcome relief. Every dormant nicotine sensor screamed to first-alert: *Welcome back! We knew you'd give in someday.*

I had begun to smoke more than ever. Two packs a day. Three packs if I got up early and stayed out late. I'd have smoked in the shower if I could have figured out a way to keep the thing lit.

I had hated myself for caving in. What had happened to all the resolve? I had resigned myself to the fact that it was better to smoke than to be fat—just the opposite of what I'd told myself before as I'd waited those endless hours for my cakes to bake. I had thought willpower was the answer—if only I were *strong* enough. I know now why that is a typical, erroneous thought of a compulsive person: "Willpower as a pure act," writes Dr. Theodore Rubin in *The Winner's Notebook,* "invariably comes from compulsive drives and contracts and further contributes to compulsion. There is no real *self* involved in an attempt to overwhelm a disastrous situation by an act of 'strength' alone. It just doesn't work. Insight, on the other hand, involves real knowing of self and real self-involvement on the deepest level."

I had no such insight into the driving force of my own inner compulsions.

Today the hard evidence against smoking is overwhelming, connecting smoking with cancer and diseases of the heart, lungs, and circulatory system. Smoking is dangerous to one's own health, to nonsmokers around, even to persons not yet born. Smoking is a problem on the job. Each year smokers miss almost three days more work than the nonsmoker. Counting smoking damage, health insurance, and other factors, the smoker costs his/her company about $4,600 per year.

Despite the almost irrefutable evidence, however, about one-third of adults—54 million Americans—are still smoking, including 26 million adult women.

Dr. Virginia Ernster, associate professor of epidemiology at the University of California at San Francisco School of Medicine, observes that cigarette companies worldwide perceive "the working woman, under stress, as the ideal candidate for their product."

Nicotine is extremely addictive; its addictive characteristics are now being compared to heroin and cocaine. What's more, although individuals involved with other addictions such as alcohol or hard drugs sometimes take a break from their usage—from a few days to weeks and sometimes even a few months—smokers never take a break. They smoke every day, through all their waking hours. Some even have difficulty making it through the night without smoking.

Dr. Ellen Gritz, director of the Division of Cancer Control at UCLA's Jonsson Comprehensive Cancer Center, points out that "cigarettes are often used to control negative moods and stressful feelings. When a woman quits, she may start expressing these negative feelings, and people around her get upset. I've had lots of women tell me that their families begged them to go back to smoking."

Even if a woman can escape this pressure, and even survive the pain and discomfort of cold-turkey withdrawal, she is met with a psychological attachment that is extremely difficult to break. Some of the following might prove helpful:

Ways To Curb The Urge To Smoke[7]

- If craving a cigarette, distract yourself, change your activity, telephone an ex-smoker or an understanding friend until the feeling subsides.

- If cigarettes give you an energy boost, try modest exercise, a brisk walk, deep breathing exercises, and a balanced diet, avoiding foods high in sugar.

- Go places where you can't smoke.

- Keep a glass of water nearby and instead of smoking take sips through a straw.

- Don't linger at the table after a meal.

- If you do slip and smoke a cigarette or two, that doesn't mean you've become a smoker again. Decide why you succumbed to temptation and set a new goal of not smoking—and not slipping up.

Remember, the urge to light up lasts only five to ten minutes.

One day I was visiting with a friend going through a painful separation. We were commiserating with each other about the messes we'd made of our lives. I took out a pack of cigarettes, my third of the day, and struggled with the stubborn cellophane wrapping.

"I'll quit if you will," she challenged me suddenly. "Let's put money on it. The first one who smokes owes the other . . . fifty dollars?"

Realizing it wouldn't be possible to extract that much in secret from my household budget, I declined the contract. "We can do it without any bets. I know we can."

Enthusiastically we pumped each other's hands. We could kick this thing. Later, to reinforce my resolve, I rolled down the window of my car as I drove home.

"Farewell, evil weeds!" I intoned, tossing the fresh pack out the window. Suddenly it was as though Karen were sitting in the car beside me. I heard her voice as I'd heard it so many times in the hospital at Warm Springs: *Please, Jesus—help me!*

"If you really exist," I whispered, "and if you really do help people . . . will you help me quit smoking? *Please.* "

When I awakened the next morning, my eyes greeted the sunny morning with a strange new clarity. And an unaccustomed sense of peace. The frayed edges of my ragged nerves were somehow knitted together. The craving for tobacco was simply and amazingly gone. I stared wonderingly through the bedroom window at the dazzling blue Big Sky of Montana.

As before, however, doing without cigarettes seemed to activate my taste buds. My urge for chocolate returned stronger than ever. I tried to resist, but defeat followed defeat in my kitchen. The inner voice seemed to gloat, *Weak, hopeless, failure.*

At the time I didn't understand that if checked in one area, the compulsive nature will break out in another, that the sickness was not this addiction or that, but deep inside me. I was upset when I went to yard sales and came home with items I didn't need, or even want. Clothing sales drew me like a moth to a flame. When closets bulged with "bargains," I hid the overflow in bags under the bed.

Harvard psychiatrist George Vaillant has observed just this kind of cross-addictive behavior, reporting that former alcoholics often shift to new dependencies—candy, compulsive work, hobbies, gambling, etc. Indeed, in the groundbreaking *Ms.* survey, women confessed addictions to a large variety of behaviors, including shopping, walking, running, yoga, exercise, cleaning, sleeping, work, daily routines, credit cards, nail-biting, even using the phone.

For me there was always a monster lying in wait, ready to take charge again: my craving for alcohol. I still sipped wine at the dinner table and drank at parties—but no longer could I count on the numbing relief, the rush of exhilaration that had always accompanied the flow of alcohol into my system. More and more often now there was only a fearful gray fog whenever I took a drink. I longed to stop altogether, but lacked the willpower—or, as Dr. Rubin points out, the self-knowledge.

The answer came unexpectedly. It was Valentine's Day, 1980. That night I was hostess for a dinner party in my home.

The day began with feelings of nervous anticipation, a desire that the party be a dazzling success. I'd made a special quilted tablecloth, spent hours planning the food—even to colors that harmonized—and arranged elaborate floral decorations.

It would be a night of striving to win the approval and acceptance of my husband's friends and law associates. I'd be under the microscope. Being scrutinized wasn't new, but an ex-mental patient always seems to have more to prove. Could I pull the evening off?

As the guests arrived, I fluttered in the kitchen, hovering over gurgling pans and checking the oven obsessively. Somehow the meal materialized on my flower- and candle-bedecked table. There were so many decorations there was barely room for the food. Profuse compliments flowed as fast as the dinner wine. Then Randall tapped his wineglass to signal "toast time."

I grasped the stem of my goblet. As I did, the dark burgundy sloshed about, creating swirling purple rings in the crystal. And in those rings I saw, as clearly as if they had been etched in the glass, three words:

Poison
Death
Insanity

I wanted to scream. I stared incredulously at the telltale words. The others were raising their glasses, laughing, talking. Couldn't they see the message inscribed in wavering purple letters?

I don't want to drink this.

I don't want to drink anything alcoholic ever again.

A feeling of warmth coursed through my body from head to toe. A renewed sense of being protected. Was it Karen's God revealing his love to me on Valentine's Day, the day for lovers?

Days passed. As with cigarettes, the craving for alcohol was startlingly and totally gone.

For other women, of course, the battle is more drawn-out, especially when they are faced with social situations in which they are urged to have "just one" drink. The following suggestions, from Hodgson and Miller's *Self-Watching: Addictions, Habits, Compulsions,* help to develop skills for coping with those social situations likely to arise:

Social Coping Strategies

1. Stay for a half hour and then leave.

2. Get over my anxiety by just listening to people. Forget about trying to impress.

3. Drink tonic, because people might think it is vodka and tonic. They will then be less likely to pressure me into drinking.

4. If I feel a craving coming on, then I'll walk around the block until it disappears—that is, the craving, not the block!

5. I must remember how good I felt at Charlie's party two months ago when I successfully resisted the pressure to drink.

6. Be assertive. Tell all and sundry that I am not drinking and I will be very angry if they offer me a drink.

Despite the fact that I had suddenly, completely lost the desire for alcohol, I had *not* lost the desire for chocolate. Or the sudden yearnings to go shopping. And the pain was still in place.

In an effort to understand my compulsive tendencies, I started reading everything I could lay my hands on. One report, "The Nature of Craving,"[8] showed that monkeys and rats, even when hungry, chose cocaine over food. When given free access to cocaine, the animals "went into a frenzy of drug-taking activity."

The study suggested that some machinery for addiction is built into our brains. To combat this innate tendency, the author called for a joining of biological, psychological, and sociological forces. No mention was made of spiritual forces having any part to play.

As I read this report, I had a picture of all the antiseptic hospital halls I'd walked down, of intellectually determined and well-meaning medical men talking in scientific jargon about my problems, of pills prescribed and then more pills, and of a kind of emotional and spiritless sterility that surrounded it all.

This sterility of spirit is referred to in Scott Peck's *The Road Less Traveled.* "It is indeed tempting for psychiatrists to view themselves as knights of modern science locked in noble combat with the destructive forces of ancient religious superstition and irrational but authoritarian dogma," he writes.

Meanwhile I struggled with the volcano of compulsion inside me. Why did eating binges and shopping splurges so quickly follow my victories over tobacco and alcohol?

I asked this question of a neighbor. Kathy was about my age, mid-forties, with a pert nose and a short, chestnut page-boy haircut. She responded by inviting me to a prayer meeting. Because I was hungry for answers, I agreed to go.

So one bright June morning I walked into a living room filled with smiling women who welcomed me warmly. Nervously I perched on the edge of a green sofa. The pastor of the Methodist church was there, giving me a sense of assurance that I was not involved with spiritual oddballs.

At the prayer meeting someone suggested that because of my exposure to the occult, I should get rid of everything related to it. I went home and burned all my occult books and horoscope readings. It was amazing the amount of psychic material a scavenger hunt revealed. I even discarded items of my clothing that had signs of the zodiac and jewelry with arcane symbols. Part of me argued that the whole performance was nothing but superstition and fanaticism. Yet with these things out of the house I felt . . . lighter, somehow. Purged.

Was it my imagination, or in the days that followed were the angry voices in my head fainter, farther off—often silent for long periods.

But the craving for food, especially chocolate, still drove me. I still slept late too many mornings, had trouble getting myself organized. My needs were visible to everyone.

Kathy, however, was one of those caring people who sees a friend through the long haul. I especially remember the morning she appeared on my doorstep clutching a book. Eyes filled with concern, she thrust the book into my hands as I stood behind the slightly cracked door.

"Here, Sand, maybe *this* will help. . . ." Then she ran back to her idling car and sped off down the street.

Shutting the door, I thrust the book into the pocket of my

rumpled bathrobe. In the walnut-framed hall mirror I caught a look at myself.

Good grief! Who is that?

Backing up in disbelief, the leering image gaped back at me. That couldn't be me! It must be some beached whale wrapped in a chenille robe.

And those haunted eyes ringed with wilted mascara. Raccoon eyes!

A beached whale with raccoon eyes.

Tears flooded my eyes, splashing down my cheeks onto my robe. I was suddenly aware of the deep hollow in my chest. I knew how to fill it. There was a fresh half-gallon of chocolate ice cream hidden in the freezer under the Brussels sprouts. I could count on my dark, cool, sweet friend to bring me relief.

To the freezer! I'd need a serving spoon. Yes, a *big* spoon. For I intended to eat it all.

The just-delivered gift of love, Kathy's book, now rested forlornly on the dark pine kitchen table, its pristine newness smudged with brown dribbles from my chocolate binge. *I'll read it tomorrow,* I promised myself.

Several weeks later Kathy's voice on the phone sounded bright and enthusiastic as she told me about an upcoming workshop at her Methodist church. I wasn't so sure, except that since I'd stopped drinking I needed something to occupy my mind. There were so many raw emotions coming to the surface that I couldn't deal with: frustration, fears, anger, and—oh, God—the guilt.

"Sandy! Welcome!" Entering the church for the workshop I was smothered with hugs of well-wishers, many of whom I'd known socially over the years in Billings. I tried not to be preoccupied with the hug wrinkles on my meticulously ironed blouse and scarf.

The workshop leaders were a couple from Spokane, Washington. As the husband spoke I glanced at the shadows on the far brick wall—a syncopated pattern of stripes. I thought of the stripes I'd seen across my lap in the hospital.

The speaker was opening his Bible. "Turn with me to Isaiah 53, verses 4 and 5," he said. Then he began reading:

"Surely he [Jesus] hath borne our griefs, and carried our sorrows: yet we did esteem him stricken, smitten of God and afflicted. But he was wounded for our transgressions, he was bruised for our iniquities . . . and by his stripes we are healed."

I stared at him open-mouthed, stunned at the timing of the words, and felt a transfusion of hope.

"Are you coming to the healing service Sunday night?" Kathy asked later. "I'll be happy to pick you up."

I shook my head. "I'd better pass it up."

Sunday evening Randall and I ate dinner in silence. I tried not to look at the kitchen clock that indicated twenty-five minutes until the healing service began. While scraping the dishes, I wondered what my priorities should be. On the one hand, my husband's negative attitude toward my churchgoing was clear. Religion almost seemed more of a threat to our marriage than my drinking. On the other hand, something inside was pushing me toward the church. That, obviously, would be a mistake.

I changed into my faded blue jeans and slipped on a baggy gray sweater for an evening of TV-watching. When I entered the den, Randall was already settled in his black leather chair, the set tuned to the Sunday night movie. I sank into the couch.

A moment later I was back on my feet. "I have to go to church," I said lamely. "I don't expect you to understand why. I'm not sure I do, either."

I raced out the front door with the image of his puzzled stare following me. Was I being driven by yet another compulsion?

Organ music was filling the church with a mighty crescendo when I entered. Such joy flooded the sanctuary that the putty in the stained glass windows must have struggled to keep them from exploding outwards.

The memory of my husband's disapproving look was dissolved in the majesty of the music. When the invitation was given to come forward for healing, I rose from my seat and walked down the center aisle. People were streaming toward the front from all over the church. There was just enough room for me to squeeze in at the altar rail.

A large white cross hung from the ceiling over the marble altar. In the brilliance of the ceiling spotlights its whiteness was dazzling. My eyes fell on the enormous open Bible resting on the marble missal stand. Below it in brushed brass letters were the words *This Do in Remembrance of Me.*

At first, as I grasped the thick oak altar rail, my mind was racing. Scenes: the living room at Uncle Ralph's; wearing the flower crown of Miss Vermont; awaiting death at my kitchen window. Places: Atlantic City, Disneyland, Deaconess Hospital here in Billings. Faces: Brad, Brent, Lisa, my mother and father, Shelly at the checkout counter, Karen. Like whirling dancers they sped past. Then calm—a holy silence.

A few minutes later a woman minister joined me at the altar rail and listened to my litany of pain. Then she placed her hands on my shoulders and looked straight into my eyes, as the following words flowed with quiet authority from her lips: "If God has forgiven all your sins, how dare you not forgive yourself?"

My eyes smarting, my nose running, I offered up my prayers to God—and felt the deep-down happiness of being accepted for what I was. I was the object of a love greater than any I had ever known.

"To forgive your own self," writes Louis B. Smedes in *Forgive and Forget*, "is almost the ultimate miracle of healing! To forgive yourself is to act out the mystery of one person who is both forgiver and forgiven. You judge yourself: this is the division within you. You forgive yourself: this is the healing of the split."

Later, as I reflected on what happened at the church, I saw it as a major step toward health. Since compulsive behavior, by its very definition, entails acts we experience as involuntary—in which our wills are overwhelmed by a desire that feels as if it comes from outside ourselves—the remedy for such behavior lies in submitting ourselves to a countervailing positive force. Alcoholics Anonymous call this force a Higher Power. Many therapists construct other ideals "outside" the patient.

A skeptic might argue that by this procedure the compulsive person merely exchanges addictions. I don't agree. Every sufferer knows the difference between pain and release from pain. As Dr. Stanton Peele writes in *Love and Addiction:*

"The difference between not being addicted and being addicted is the difference between seeing the world as your arena and seeing the world as your prison. . . . If what a person is engaged in enhances his ability to live—if it enables him to work more effectively, to love more beautifully, to appreciate the things around him more, and finally, if it allows him to grow, to change, and expand—then it is not addictive."

Though other compulsive women may find other "Higher Powers" that release them from enslavement to detested but irresistible urges, I can speak authentically about only one. For me, Christian conversion and faith was the necessary outside force to break the grip of patterns that held me in thrall most of my life.

A sociologist might say that compulsive individuals in our culture are predisposed toward a Judeo-Christian solution to their behavior. Whatever reasons may be given, I can only say personally that it worked for me. My compulsive lifestyle was reordered by a power outside myself, which since that night in the church I continue to experience and call Jesus Christ.

Intervention

For some reason, I can tell you where each person in that room was sitting; the floor plan is burned into my brain. . . . And they all proceeded to confront me with a second intervention. Only this time, they meant business. . . . All of them hurt me. I collapsed into tears. But I still had enough sense to realize they hadn't come around just to make me cry; they were there because they loved me and wanted to help me.

—Betty Ford
The Times of My Life

*A*s I PROBE BACK INTO MY RECOVERY, AND THAT OF OTHER COMPULSIVE people, and see how the sick and defeated are transformed into healthy and productive people, one central fact comes through: *Recovery seldom comes about through one or two experiences; recovery is not an event, it is a process.*

Encountering Karen at Warm Springs Hospital was a beginning, the activation of a long-buried desire to respond to the hurt and need of someone else. Explains John Schwarzlose, executive director and vice-president of the Betty Ford Center: "Alcoholics and addicts have isolated themselves for years. We want them to form relationships again."

The discovery of those three little words *Do it now* was also a step to healing, the coming to life of a part of me that wanted to take responsibility. It too was part of the process.

After throwing my cigarettes from the car window and uttering what might have been the first real prayer of my life, I was loosed from bondage to nicotine. When months later I was released from the desire to drink at the Valentine's Day party, I thought I was now free from all addiction. (Far from it. My compulsions to overeat and go on shopping binges were to reemerge stronger than ever.)

And after the beautiful cleansing experience at the Billings Methodist Church, the mental and physical listlessness brought on by years of abusing my body was replaced by a powerful infusion of energy. I felt more alive than I had in twenty years. Yet this healing was also only a step on the long road back to health.

During the recovery process, I encountered attitudes that were troubling. Some new church friends took the position that I would find all the healing I needed through prayer alone. God's work in me might be endangered, they said, if I got involved with any secular-scientific treatment. The medical world, on the other hand, expressed indifference and even hostility toward any healing that came about through "religion," saying it came either from mass hysteria or a kind of self-hypnosis.

Yet I could see value in what both camps offered.

In any case, there were few effective medical treatment centers for addictive people until the 1970s. Before then alcoholics and drug addicts were often institutionalized, as I had been, right in with the mentally disturbed. Once separate facilities were set up to help addiction sufferers, a new era began. These medical centers usually worked closely with Alcoholics Anonymous (AA), the one approach to alcoholism that had proven effective statistically since it was started in 1935. A significant discovery was that the basic Twelve-Step program of AA worked not only for alcoholics, but for other compulsive behavior problems, too. (See p. 209.)

Recovery begins, counselors discovered, when patients face reality—as required by the all-important First Step of the program. But oh, how hard it is for the addict to change years of practiced deception and self-delusion. Our emotions are defensive, self-protective. Facing truth can be like pulling teeth without anesthesia . . . as I was soon to discover.

For weeks after my healing at the Methodist church, Bible study and prayer groups became the doors to a new life, while I tried not to look at the wreckage of two homes.

My three teenage children were living with their father and had their own lives and activities, where I did not fit. Randall and I were growing farther and farther apart. Many months had passed since my last drink. My resolve was intact, but my body was behaving strangely. Sometimes I talked like a machine gun. I raced from the supermarket to a prayer meeting to back home again at a frantic pace.

"Are you sure you're okay?" friends would ask. "You seem so revved up. Slow down and catch up with yourself!"

Any sense of peace had lit momentarily like the butterfly that had enchanted me in my childhood hideaway, then flitted off elusively. A restless gnawing often filled my heart. I couldn't seem to focus my mind anymore. Blaming the symptoms on the stress of my personal life, I didn't realize I was heading straight for a "dry drunk" condition when a recovering alcoholic exhibits deceptive, unrealistic or "hyper" behavior without the use of alcohol. (See Checklist of Symptoms, p. 214.)

Thinking a change of scene would help, I decided to drive out to a seminar in Seattle. On the way I could spend the weekend with my new friend Cathy and her husband, Dirk.

At their home in Red Lodge, Montana, Cathy and Dirk welcomed me warmly. Feeling exhilarated by our evening of discussion, I lingered in the cozy living room of their log cabin lodge long after Cathy and Dirk went off to bed.

Classical music from an FM station set a dreamy mood. I drifted about the room, rolled back the braided rugs, and danced barefoot on the smooth varnished floor.

The sound of a male voice fractured my reverie. It was Dirk. "What in the world are you doing at this ungodly hour?"

Startled, I just stared at him.

"Sit down, Sandy. I want to talk to you,' he exclaimed as he tightened the tie of his terrycloth bathrobe. "You may not like what I'm going to say, but I have to say it anyway."

He studied me for a moment in the soft light. "I know how much progress you've made since Cathy and I first met you and how fragile you are right now, but I have to tell you that your behavior is absolutely bonkers. You are on one heck of an emotional binge, kiddo. A dry drunk. If you don't do something about it, it may turn into a wet drunk and God knows what would happen to you then.

"You are in absolutely *no* condition to drive to Seattle by yourself. Or anywhere else for that matter. You need to go to a treatment center. And fast. I mean tomorrow. Before the sun goes down.

"Meanwhile, quit prancing around like a princess and get to bed. You need rest. We'll call St. Mary's when the office opens at eight o'clock and see if we can get you in. You've got to go, Sandy. Your life depends on it. You're a lot sicker than you think you are."

I hated him. I was fine . . . just on a slight roll. I argued, stormed, wept, but deep down I knew he was right. His words pierced through all my denial. I couldn't run any longer. My life was still out of control. It was time to face my sickness head-on. Dirk helped me face the truth—that I needed professional help.

The next day I was on my way to St. Mary's Treatment Center in Minneapolis.

The "dry drunk" is a common experience for recovering addicts if there has been no inner healing of the emotions. The message to me was pointed: "You may have stopped drinking, Sandy, but you are still binging emotionally." My compulsive nature was still in control. Turn off tobacco, turn on sweets; turn off alcohol, turn on a "spiritual" high from music or overtalk.

What Dirk had done for me was a spontaneous form of an increasingly popular treatment approach called *intervention*. (See p. 258.) The purpose: to get the sick person to face up to reality. The method: confrontation. "Your behavior is bonkers, Sandy. Your very life's at stake. Get to treatment—fast."

Intervention is "a move initiated out of love and concern by the people who care about the alcoholic," writes Mary Ellen Pinkham in *How to Stop the One You Love from Drinking*. "It involves their getting together to tell the alcoholic the facts about his disease and how it is affecting him. It's the only kind, gentle, and caring way to help a chemically dependent person. It's the only thing that works, the key to stopping someone whose life is in danger."

If too many family members have been "co-dependents" with the addict for too long a period, they lose their ability to be honest with each other, to share true feelings. An intervention reverses this process of denial and deception by the family and facilitates their facing up to truth—and dealing with their loved one—in a loving, caring way.

Since family and close contacts are too involved emotionally to lead an intervention, a specialist is needed. Such a professional can usually be found through a local drug or alcohol council, Alcoholics Anonymous, or a mental health department.

Interventions are structured carefully, with as many as six or more people involved. The ideal combination is the spouse, a parent, one or more children, a doctor, the employer, and the family pastor.

Preparation for an intervention calls for a series of meetings between family members and the intervention professional, usually at a location other than the addict's home. The professional explains the process and rehearses the concerned persons as to how they will present their facts. Very often this is the first time the family has actually sat down together and discussed what is going on in the home. All those involved make a list of events in which the addict's behavior has hurt and embarrassed them. Then they practice their presentation. Intervention works for drug abuse, bulimia, anorexia, gambling, and other compulsive behaviors.

Other suggestions:[9]

Timing is crucial. Most successful interventions take place early in the morning when the addict is most vulnerable. It is not advisable to do an intervention when the addict has had time to fortify herself with alcohol or drugs. This is when her denial and defenses are highest.

Firmness of resolve. The spouse and family should have a plan for separating themselves from the addict if she refuses to go for treatment. The employer should be ready with an ultimatum: treatment or loss of job. Often the threat of the loss of one's salaried position is the most persuasive factor.

Who to exclude from an intervention. Anyone who would be too legalistic or moralistic; anyone whose mental balance is questionable; family members too full of hate to perceive the addict as sick and in need of help.

Have a specific treatment plan ready. If the addict agrees to go for treatment, have a time and place firmly set. If there is too much delay, the addict will change her mind.

If the intervention fails. Sometimes the addict will storm out of the meeting. If possible, try it again. Remember that there is tremendous anxiety inside the addict, who is involved in all-out denial. What doesn't work at one setting, will at another. Also the intervention, even if it fails, can start a healing process in the family by bringing members together to face the truth of their situation.

Is there any type of person for whom intervention won't work? None that I know of. When I went to a treatment center, I met doctors, pastors, two lawyers, and a judge, all of whom were patients. Addiction grips people in the highest and lowest job classifications—which is why Betty Ford in *A Glad Awakening* calls alcoholism an "equal-opportunity disease."

There is new hope for all these people in that ninety-seven percent of alcoholics, given the intervention procedure by a specialist, go to treatment within forty-eight hours. The process is so simple that few can believe it works—but it does.

I hated being confronted by Dirk just as much as I had three years before by my friend Lois Ann. For this was the second (not the first) time someone had cared enough to play this uncongenial but necessary role in my life. Three years earlier, at the height of my involvement with the Serenity Society, when each new "spiritual counselor" sent me spiraling deeper into craziness and depression, Lois Ann had organized her own version of intervention.

One day she'd invited me to her house for morning coffee to meet a special friend. The friend turned out to be a vivacious blonde who had just gotten out of an alcohol rehabilitation center in Minneapolis. Her sky-blue eyes danced as she excitedly related her twenty-eight day experience there. "I feel like a new woman," she rhapsodized, "like I have a second chance in life. I can't believe how much better I feel."

I took an instant dislike to this lovely creature. She looked too happy, too put together. I suddenly felt terribly tacky in the tired black polyester pantsuit I'd had on for several days. My head itched from need of a shampoo; the runners in my pantyhose looked like the Los Angeles Freeway. *What a slob you are,* I had thought to myself.

Lois Ann cleared her deep voice and began in halting phrases. "I've invited you here today for a very specific reason, Sandy. I don't know much about alcohol, but perhaps this is your problem, too. Perhaps you need treatment. I can't bear to see what you're doing to yourself. . . ." Taking a deep breath as though to muster a new burst of courage, she added painfully, "Have you looked at yourself in a mirror lately?"

Her words burned into my soul. She had hit a raw nerve. But alcohol wasn't my problem! I drank to escape my problems.

"I'll be glad to phone and make arrangements for you," the friend volunteered. "I know a marvelous counselor there who can answer any questions you might have."

Soon I was chatting with a pleasant-voiced older man. "We'll take good care of you here, Sandy," he said. "When you get out, you'll be the woman your husband fell in love with."

That challenge registered. I promised Lois Ann I'd speak with my psychiatrist and my husband. At my doctor's appointment that afternoon, I broached the subject. He thought it was worth a try. The sessions with him were clearly not working.

Randall was more skeptical. The last three years had diminished his faith for my restoration. He saw such devastation and hopelessness in me. He lived with it and in it. Nevertheless, he agreed it was worth trying.

One January morning in 1977 I was on a Northwest jet headed for Minneapolis.

The intervention set up by Lois Ann had succeeded to the extent that it got me into a treatment center. In the majority of cases today, these specialized facilities get the addict turned around. I was one of their failures. The twenty-eight-day treatment, like my short stays on the psychiatric floor of Billings' Deaconess Hospital, removed me temporarily from my destructive lifestyle and started me on new disciplines. But when I returned home and tried to deal with the old problems, the old pitfalls were too many. I chose to ignore the "aftercare" plan that had been set up for me. I'd been confronted with the truth, but at that period in my life I had had no resources to undergird me and I couldn't cope with it. I had opted for the "out" of suicide and begun squirreling away sleeping pills on a closet shelf.

Perhaps, though, it was that first intervention by Lois Ann in 1977 that prepared me for this second one, in June 1980, which got me into a treatment program that worked.

Facing Truth

Contrition . . . is not an American virtue, and, indeed, mere contrition could admit everything, and change nothing. To find culprits is more our style; but culprits, in taking their punishment, take our part of the guilt with them. Liberation can come only from insights into the relevance of past guilt and into the place of ethical choice in the reformation of identity.

Erik H. Erikson, M.D.
Dimensions of a New Identity

LOOKING BACK, I SOMETIMES THINK DIRK'S INTERVENTION, UNSTRUCtured as it was, saved my life. I had been trying to put up a good front with Randall, my children, and my friends; underneath I was confused and frightened. What to do about my marriage? Though Randall had supported me during six bad years, I had sensed his rejection in a number of ways. Now that I'd stopped drinking and was on the road to recovery, he expected me to fit back into his lifestyle. I couldn't do it. It was this social scenario that had kept me in trouble for so long.

"In our society," writes Betty Ford in *The Times of My Life*, "we get to know one another over drinks, we associate feasts and celebrations with liquor. We think we have to drink, that it's a social necessity. . . . It's romantic as long as you can handle it—for years I could and did—but it's misery when you become addicted."

Randall didn't understand this, or why my new religious faith was suddenly important. Since I was no longer the wife he married, and since we were going in different directions, we agreed to separate.

My children were completely bewildered by my decision to go to a treatment center. To them, I was more stable than they could ever remember me. Why did I have to go back to the hospital? I couldn't explain to them how desperately insecure I was, how close to the breaking point.

In mid-June 1980, I entered St. Mary's Rehabilitation Center, a twenty-eight-day treatment facility for alcohol and drug-related addictions in Minneapolis (a different facility than the one I'd gone to three years earlier).

The three-story treatment center contains, in addition to patients' rooms and counselors' offices, a number of small meeting lounges, a large lecture room, a small chapel with stained glass windows, nurses' stations, and a large recreation area with pool tables and a piano.

I had a small single room with cream painted walls, a hospital bed, and built-in dresser and desk. The daily schedule given us:

Breakfast, 8:00 A.M.
Morning lecture, 9:00 A.M.
Group therapy, 10:00–11:45 A.M.
Lunch, 12:00 noon
Afternoon lecture, 1:00 P.M.
Group therapy, 2:00–4:30 P.M.
Free time/ relaxation therapy, 4:30–6:00 P.M.
Dinner, 6:00 P.M.
Evening lecture, 7:00 P.M.
Free time/alcohol support group meetings/reading/homework, 8:30 on

At intake I was given a physical, a blood test, and psychological testing (Minnesota Multiphasic Personality Inventory—the "MMPI"). I also met with a staff psychiatrist who suggested Lithium therapy for my mood swings. For the first few days my blood pressure was monitored frequently.

For me, group therapy would be the cutting edge of the program. Six of us met together twice a day for close sharing led by a staff counselor. In our group there was Gwen, our counselor, in her late forties; Max, a stockbroker, maybe sixty; Carol, fiftyish, a clothing saleswoman; Larry, a balding, middle-aged businessman; Sue, a tense, depressed girl barely twenty; and myself, now forty-four.

We met in Gwen's office, a plain room with a desk pushed into the corner and six plastic chairs placed in a circle. On one wall hung a chart of the Twelve Steps of Alcoholics Anonymous. I got as far as the First Step—"We admitted we were powerless over alcohol, that our lives had become unmanageable"—and stopped reading. *Powerless. Unmanageable.* Tough words.

Gwen passed out a worksheet to each of us. Homework to be done in our rooms that evening. In response to a series of questions we were to write out our drinking history. I did not look forward to that. "You need to get the garbage in your lives out on the floor and sort through it," Gwen explained. "You will know if you're in touch with how it really was, because it will hurt. So I wish you a lot of pain, because then something is happening to you."[10]

After two hours of sharing and teaching, Gwen closed the session. Holding hands in a circle, we recited Reinhold Niebuhr's Serenity Prayer (a staple in many treatment programs): "God grant me the serenity to accept the things I cannot change, the courage to change the things I can, and the wisdom to know the difference."

That night I sat down to tackle the homework. *The sooner I get going,* I told myself, *the sooner I'll get it over with.* At the little formica-topped desk, I began reading the sheet of questions.

"Effects on character. List thirty values important to you and give examples of how you have compromised them as a result of your usage."

Suddenly my mind was swirling with indictments—ignoring people's feelings, lying, wasting money, forgetting my children's needs, taking advantage. . . . Now the whirlpool was sucking me down toward unbearable horrors. I flipped the sheet of paper over and slapped my hand down on top of it. "I'll do it later."

I wandered into the big lounge and joined Carol, the fiftyish clothing salesperson, and Sue, the depressed twenty-year-old. "It's so awful to be a woman and an alcoholic," Carol was saying. "The hiding you have to do, the denying—it really grinds your insides."

Sue nodded bleakly.

"What made me really mad was the unfairness," Carol continued. "It was okay for the men to be at the bar having fun. I was stuck at home. My husband and I had equal status till we got married, and then all of a sudden, *plop*!"

I nodded, remembering my days at Pepsi Cola: "I wanted to drink like a man so I could be with the men."

Our group sessions, while the cutting edge of the program, soon became the most difficult part of treatment for me. There was always a knot in my stomach as I approached the door to our counselor's room. How could I escape Gwen's penetrating green eyes? I admired her, but feared she could make mincemeat of my carefully cultivated poise if she probed too close. I would sit in the circle with my best Miss America training: knees and ankles together, one foot tucked behind the other. And my Miss America smile intact. I'd learned to smile early. "Put on a happy face," my mother would tell me.

When my turn came to give a brief biography, I described my hospital experiences in Billings and Warm Springs, and how I'd since stopped smoking and drinking. I touched lightly on my healing that night at the Methodist church, trying hard not to come across as a religious fanatic. Most of the group looked impressed with my progress. Gwen's eyes were expressionless.

"You paint a positive picture of yourself, Sandy. Just why are you here?" Gwen asked.

"My friends think I'm on a dry drunk."

"Do you agree with them?"

"I guess so."

"But you're not sure?"

"My life is sort of a mess. My marriage is breaking up; that is, my second marriage. My three children are living with their father, my first husband. And"—to my disgust, tears were filling my eyes—"and I'm . . . well, not sure of myself at all."

"In short, you could fall off the wagon tomorrow."

"I guess so. I came here to Minneapolis for treatment back in 1977. Stayed sober for two months afterwards, then took that one drink. I know I shouldn't drink."

"Correction. You know you can't drink, but you're not sure you won't."

"I'm pretty sure."

"Sandy, I'll be blunt with you. In some ways you're the sickest person in this room. You spout pious phrases, you hold people off with your sense of humor and your light approach, but you're not in touch with your feelings. I've yet to hear you say how you feel."

"Right now I feel like I've been kicked in the butt."

"Good."

"And I'm miserable underneath all these smiles." The tears were flowing again. "And I'm scared. And I hate myself for what I've done to my family."

"Much better, Sandy. For the first time you come across as real." She turned to others in the group. "What is your feedback to Sandy?"

"Likable, but too pious," ventured Carol. "I felt she was determined to show us she didn't belong here."

"Trying too hard," offered Max. "She was out to win us from the start. A people-pleaser. A lot of froth on top to cover up something underneath she didn't want us to see."

"Hear that, Sandy." Gwen's eyes were boring into me. "Because you've been to treatment before and because you've been dry for a while, you felt you were above the others."

Devastating. Carol handed me some tissues. I felt naked before these people.

Inner healing had begun.

The purpose of these group sessions was to get us to open up, be honest, be vulnerable, express what we felt, not what we thought we ought to feel. At the next session, Gwen zeroed in on my relationship to Randall. "How did he react to your drinking?"

"Frustration at first. Apathy at the end. As a lawyer it bugged him that he couldn't persuade me to stop. He's used to being able to control people and situations."

"So you showed him that he couldn't control you by drinking more than ever."

I shifted uneasily in my chair. "My drinking was a problem before I married him."

"Would you have drunk so much if he had been less controlling?" Max asked suddenly.

Startled, I thought a moment. "Maybe not," I admitted.

Max kept pressing, "Why?"

I jammed my hands under my thighs. "Well, I got so mad . . . maybe there was some revenge mixed in there."

"I just heard something honest," Gwen said, "and I congratulate you. What was your reward for getting mad?"

My mind swam. My mouth was dry. Leaning forward, I stared at the toes of my shoes. Maybe if I leaned far enough the floor would open and swallow me. "I don't know. Maybe I was getting something out of my system."

"There was a great big reward," Gwen said, "and I'm not sure you want to give it up yet."

I could feel the circle of eyes watching me. Finally I said tentatively, "Maybe part of the reward was an inner permission to drink more."

"Part?" asked Gwen, cocking an eyebrow.

"A lot," I said.

"Do you see," Gwen said, "that your anger has been one of the dynamics of your alcoholism?"

There was another long pause. I felt a fear I could not explain. "But sometimes I drank because I was happy."

Max asked, "What would make you so happy you'd take a drink?"

I laughed. "Not taking a drink."

Gwen was not smiling. "I don't know whether you do that in all your relationships, but humor is a way of getting off the hook and stopping communication. As I see it, Max was trying to help and you made a joke. Then he's down and you're up. Take a look at that."

Gwen spoke again. "I urge you to accept what has been said, Sandy. I don't see you making any progress toward accepting the disease concept and the fact that you are powerless over alcohol— which tells me that you are not working on your First Step. You will not really get into treatment until you begin focusing on *you,* your addiction, and how it has affected you."

At the close of the session I hurried away to an isolated chair in the second-floor lounge. I replayed the last exchange—Gwen's voice zapping me for that joke. I felt marooned in a hot funk of embarrassment, like a little girl caught red-handed.

Max's voice broke into my trance. "Sandy, don't look so down. It happens to the best of us."

Looking up, I smiled ruefully. "It's always darkest before it's totally black." Max shrugged and left me alone.

I felt a flush like a prickly rash spreading up my throat and across my face. I had just done it again, made a quip to keep someone at arm's length.

My time came as it did for everyone in our group to read aloud the first homework assignment: a comprehensive look at how addiction had affected every area of my life. Afterward, I waited confidently for the group's approval. No one could accuse me now of covering up: I'd bared my very soul!

But the others disagreed. Some thought I'd minimized the effects on myself and my family, others that I "skated away" from talking about real issues.

And I was totally unprepared for Gwen's response. She told me calmly that I was one of the angriest women she had ever had in her group and that I'd better get in touch with that anger or it would surely sabotage my recovery. "When you finish your treatment here," she said, "I think you should consider going to a women's halfway house for continuing recovery."

She added that I'd been so ill for the past twenty years, I hardly knew what planet I was on, and that going to Billings could be disastrous. "And from now on," she concluded, "I want your outsides to match your insides! No more hiding behind your smile."

I was stunned that she detected such anger in me. I hadn't lost my cool even once in the group. Was I really so angry? I wasn't sure I wanted to find out.

After this session, I slipped down to the chapel on the second floor of the treatment center. It was my special place of peace and refuge, an eye of calm in the storm all around me. Kneeling in the serenity of that place, I started to search my life for clues to my aborted anger.

As I meditated, I saw I was indeed angry, and that it had begun when I was very young. I had picked up people's feelings and moods, known what was acceptable behavior and what was not.

Observing adult responses to my actions, I'd discovered it was not all right to be angry. My home was not a healthy emotional climate where feelings were expressed frankly. So I learned to mask anger and annoyance, smile sweetly, say nothing. I felt one way and acted another. Pretty soon I didn't know how I felt. Apparently this pattern was still in effect, refined by years of practice. My denial system protected me like a bulletproof vest.

What Gwen said, then, was true. Beneath the placid exterior I was angry. In fact, I was mad as hell! A childhood episode came back to me. Once when I was angry at my grandmother I'd covered my whole body with big white adhesive-tape Band-Aids. Then I'd stood in the lawn sprinkler so the Mercurochrome on the pads would run down my body like blood. It was a pathetic attempt to get people to notice my feelings—and won me no attention at all.

As an adult I became a door-slammer. On three occasions, when angry at my husband, I'd thrown pots through a kitchen window. The man at the glass repair shop chuckled the third time he replaced the pane: "It'd be cheaper to kick a tire, lady."

I had never learned to express feelings appropriately. I knew I couldn't blame my parents. They were victims of victims and I realized that I, too, had made victims of my children.

Was it this pattern of denied emotions, I wondered, generation after generation, that had made me such a ready receptor for those "angry little men" who'd tormented me so long? I only knew there was an avalanche of rage inside that wanted to come out.

A similar pattern of repressed anger shows up again and again in compulsive individuals like me—smiling people-pleasers who are covering up years of suppressed anger and hurt.

"No matter how 'grown-up' one acts in therapy or in life," writes Arthur Janov in *The Primal Scream,* "it must be an act which has little bearing on one's maturity until the 'little girl' is felt. . . . We must feel the anger fully in order to eradicate it. When a person can feel himself, instead of acting out his feelings symbolically, he will be unlikely to act either impulsively or aggressively. The dialectic of anger, as with Pain, is that when it is felt, it disappears, when it is not felt, it remains waiting to be felt."

As the days passed and I opened up haltingly to the group, some of the long-buried feelings came out. Memories surfaced that had festered unacknowledged for years. But always, it seemed, more pain lay underneath.

The third week of my treatment was called "family week," made memorable for me by a visit from my son Brent, at nineteen a handsome six-footer. My middle child, Brent has always been creative, athletic, popular with his peers. The day he joined our group, Gwen placed our two chairs in the center of the circle face-to-face, then asked Brent to describe how it felt to grow up in an alcoholic home.

He shifted about uncomfortably and said he hadn't noticed anything was wrong until he had visited the homes of his friends and seen that their mothers didn't drink as I did.

Gwen explained to him that children of alcoholics blank out the pain and have almost an amnesia about their parents' drinking.

As Brent talked, I looked into his guileless eyes and felt such a wrenching pain in my stomach that I thought I would be sick. The sense of lost years with him, Brad, and Lisa was almost unbearable.

"Stop crying, Sandy," Gwen ordered. "You're manipulating him with your tears."

It was a hard time, I know, for Brent, as it was for me—yet so very good to have him there.

After kissing him goodbye as he left for the airport, I returned to my room and found a note propped up against my pillow. It was neatly printed with a black felt-tip pen on a paper towel:

Dear Mom, I am sorry that my stay had to be so short. I hope that we have cleared up some problems that you have had! I learned a lot while I was here. The people are beautiful. I want you to know I *love* you very much and I don't use the term loosely. I'm sure Brad and

Lisa feel the same. Please give my best wishes to all the nice friends of yours. I send them all the willpower in the world and my very best wishes. Take care and if you ever have a problem, just give us a call. We will help.

Love, Brent
& God bless

I weep seven years later upon reading this. The message has been framed and matted in sunny yellow and hangs on my kitchen wall. It's a precious prized treasure from the heart of my son.

During treatment I was served with divorce papers. Though I knew they were coming, the reality devastated me. More guilt, remorse, defeat. For two days I barely functioned. The lecture by a counselor named Jessica was life-restoring.

Jessica had been a Roman Catholic nun, then an alcoholic. She'd found sobriety through the AA program and was now dedicated to carrying the message of restoration to others. Her very presence inspired confidence. The serenity of her spirit washed over me as she began to speak.

"An alcoholic can be sober," Jessica was saying, "but still the most miserable, God-forsaken person on two feet. There has to be some rebuilding of the spiritual values destroyed by chemicals: honesty, humility, forgiveness, trust, love, courage. This process begins with surrender. It is saying 'I give up!' I surrender to the powerlessness and unmanageability of my life. The chemical controlled me. I said and did things while drunk that were hurtful, painful, devastating, destructive.

"In recovery," she continued, "the hardest thing for me to accept was the fact that kind, gentle, caring Jessica, while drunk, was capable of doing terrible things. I knew I could be forgiven for those things. But as long as I was unable or unwilling to forgive myself, it was difficult to feel their forgiveness in my gut. I still carried the burden of my past around like a big boulder on my back."

As Jessica spoke my thoughts went back to that night at the Methodist church. The words of the woman minister rang in my head: "If God has forgiven all your sins, how dare you not forgive yourself?" It sounded so simple, but I saw now that a lack of self-forgiveness had continued to be the biggest stumblingblock in my recovery.

Jessica continued: "So I finally faced the reality that I was a failure at running my own affairs. Then the question: Where am I going to get help outside myself? Is there anything in this program that I can grab hold of and hang onto very, very tightly that will make me become a healthier, happier person? Is there anything that will give me a deep sense of forgiveness? That brought me to a further stage of surrender—surrender to God as I understood him—which, surprisingly, I had never really done.

"I know now," Jessica concluded, "that God will give me the grace, the strength, the courage, the people that I need to get through today without drinking. For that I am very grateful."

Powerlessness. Acceptance. Surrender. Gratitude. Great words to say, but how to own them, to integrate them into my life? I suddenly saw with new eyes the unmanageability of my life.

I could take Step One of our recovery program and put any number of things where the word *alcohol* appears: cigarettes, food, relationships, shopping sprees, the occult, caffeine, anger. . . .* The list seemed endless. I was powerless over my whole life. That was what was unmanageable.

Step Two was equally crucial: "Came to believe that a power greater than myself could restore me to sanity."

"Developing your spirituality," writes Robin Norwood in *Women Who Love Too Much*, "no matter what your religious orientation, basically means *letting go of self-will,* of the determination to make

---

* The Twelve Steps can be applied to any self-help group or program.

things happen the way you think they should . . . believing that you alone have all the answers . . . becoming willing to hold still, be open, and wait for guidance for yourself. It means learning to let go of fear (all of the 'what ifs') and despair (all of the 'if onlys') and replacing them with positive thoughts and statements about your life."

At the end of her talk, Jessica instructed us to stand and grasp the hands of the people next to us while we sang "Amazing Grace." At my right was a ruddy-faced young man whose mother, Carol, was in my treatment group. At my left was Veronica, a tiny, birdlike woman in treatment for her ninth time. I was struck by the difference of handclasps. One so powerful, the other so tremulous. The words we sang pierced my soul: "I once was lost, but now am found, was blind, but now I see."

Soon people were sobbing openly. Veronica leaned against me, her tears wetting the sleeve of my blue cotton shirt. I doubt there was a person in that room who was not grappling with that reality. There was new purpose in faces that before had been vacant. The air was charged with electricity. I felt safe and cared for and loved. But most of all, I felt forgiven.

Self-forgiveness without honesty, writes Louis B. Smedes in *Forgive and Forget*, "is psychological hocus-pocus. The rule is: we cannot really forgive ourselves unless we look at the failure in our past and call it by its right name. When you forgive yourself, you rewrite your script. What you are in your present scene is not tied down to what you did in an earlier scene. . . . You release yourself today from yesterday's scenario. You walk into tomorrow, guilt gone."

12

Anger and Male Dependency

> *At our worst, we women who love too much are relationship addicts, "man junkies" strung out on pain, fear, and yearning. . . . We use relationships in the same way that we use our addictive substance: to take our pain away. . . . As long as we are bent on escaping ourselves and avoiding our pain, we stay sick. The harder we try and the more avenues of escape we pursue, the sicker we get as we compound addictions with obsessions.*
>
> Robin Norwood
> *Women Who Love Too Much*

A S MORE AND MORE IS LEARNED ABOUT ADDICTIVE BEHAVIOR, THERAPISTS are urging patients to continue their recovery programs beyond the twenty-eight-day average stay at a treatment center, preferably in a halfway house. If for one reason or another, often financial, this is impossible, the alternative is a support group in the patient's hometown using the Twelve-Step program.

At the suggestion of Gwen, my counselor at the treatment center, I agreed to enter a halfway house. Twenty years of addictive behavior, she said, could not be changed in a month's program. I hated to be away still longer from Billings where I could see my children several times a week, but my prime responsibility to my family was to get well.

My interview at the Jane Dickman House (about twenty miles outside of St. Paul) was a surprise. The words *halfway house* had always conjured up a vision of cracked plaster walls, leaky ceilings, and dead flies on the windowsills. In contrast, the ride up to Dickman House coursed along a winding driveway, passed a tennis court and manicured lawn, and came to a halt beneath the portico of a sprawling wood-and-stone structure. It looked more like a country vacation resort than a facility for chemically dependent women.

Inside I was led past groups of women talking over coffee around small tables and into a dining room with a chalet window that offered a panoramic view of a lake. My interviewer asked me probing questions about my life and my goals for recovery, noting my answers on a yellow pad. At the end of our time, she offered a treatment plan for me: I needed to work on building trust levels, improving family relationships, understanding my feelings and emotions. The cost of living there came to about $1,100 a month. All participants were encouraged to find jobs locally or in nearby St. Paul, not only to help pay expenses, but to build a new life of independence.

The first few weeks were spent in "Feelings Groups," large and small house meetings, one-on-one counseling, exercise periods, and alcohol support group meetings. There were kitchen duties, special weekend projects, and social events with our brother halfway house, Team House, in nearby St. Paul.

Each woman at Jane Dickman was given a "verbal" by her counselor. Before we were allowed to speak, we had to use our special verbal and say how we felt. Mine, for example, was, "I need to share with you on a meaningful level. I feel sad [or embarrassed, or angry, or whatever]." By doing this, I would be forced to get in touch with my feelings.

After one group session my counselor, a no-nonsense, authoritative woman named Betsy, called me into her office for a one-on-one.

"Sandy, your steady smile tells me that you're a good-natured person. Are you really that happy on the inside or have you gone through life in a smiling depression?"

"Perhaps."

"Then that happy smile must be a mask to cover up how you're really feeling."

I nodded, recalling how my group at St. Mary's had called me on this.

"Some of your smiles seem spontaneous and natural. Others I suspect are cover-ups."

"Cover-ups for what?" I asked, half-afraid to hear her response.

"Your deep-rooted anger. We're going to deal with that in the next few weeks."

With that, Betsy instructed the other women to confront me every time I smiled and ask what I was smiling about. As an exercise to get my insides to match my outsides, I was to pay a small fine whenever I used my smile as a defense. I was also to be penalized if I employed exaggerated words like *itsy-bitsy, teeny, humongous, gigantic.* Such words distorted communication, Betsy said. It was a shock to discover how often these exaggerations popped out in my everyday conversation.

Betsy also assigned me individual "anger work." I was to spend five minutes a day in the indoor racquetball court "screaming." At first this exercise seemed ridiculous. Self-conscious at first, my screams were little more than squeaks, but as I got into the routine, the emotion poured out. Using the ball as the object of my anger, I blasted at it with my racquet. Soon the squeaks became roars. I discovered I was not merely angry, but as Gwen had predicted, I was full of buried rage.

If the resident had an automobile, as I did, those of us with anger work were encouraged to use driving time for screaming. Once, on my way back to Dickman House from doing an errand, I was idling at a stoplight and decided it would be a good place to let out some feelings. I didn't realize my car window was open until a woman in the lane next to me scrambled from her car to come to my aid. That cured me from screaming at stoplights, but not on interstates.

Betsy suggested I make an anger diary going back as far as I could remember, noting events, people, and situations that made me angry. What a revelation that was! I'd had emotional gangrene most of my life and never realized it.

I'd always been one of those "don't-make-waves" people who shied away from confrontations. In our sexual abuse group one day I was urged to deal with my unexpressed anger against Uncle Ralph for his molestation of me when I was five.

"Go back to that place and that episode," the counselor instructed. "Tell your uncle how it was for you. You're not the helpless little girl now. Tell him whatever you need to." She gave me several pillows to use.

Closing my eyes for concentration, I went back in time to Uncle Ralph's living room. I could smell the Sir Walter Raleigh tobacco he rolled into homemade cigarettes . . . hear the sound of ticking clocks from the hallway.

Then I saw Uncle Ralph sitting in his squeaky wooden rocker. Felt his hands on me, heard him wheezing, clicking his teeth. I started to sob and beat my thighs.

"Use the pillows," the counselor ordered.

"I loved and trusted you, Uncle Ralph, and you took advantage of me. I was little and couldn't fight back. You hurt me! You scared me! I hate you for that!"

I was shouting now, my voice high and shrill. The five-year-old Sandy was doubled over, pounding the pillows with both fists.

During these sessions I realized that in the past my anger had erupted all right, only in indirect, inappropriate ways. Example: *overeating.* You could never have convinced me when I was binging on chocolate that I was really acting out my inner rage. Not just at Uncle Ralph, but at all the times I'd swallowed my feelings and said nothing. It made no difference that my dress size was headed for the twenties, that I was totally revulsed at myself and nauseated physically by food. The raging dragon inside demanded to be fed. Or placated with cigarettes. Or booze. Or a new outfit.

One day the staff counselor at Dickman House jolted me by saying, "Sandy, do you realize how male-dependent you are?"

Anger in me was now very near the surface; *available* was the staff's approving term. It welled up in me. "You make me sound like a streetwalker!" I flared.

"I'm not talking about that kind of dependency. Your thoughts, your actions, your needs are centered on men. You require their approval to be fulfilled."

"How can you say that?" I argued. "I've been hurt by men all my life. Now at long last I'm free of them."

The counselor shook her head. "You only think you're free. Let me explain what I mean." She tapped a paper on her desk.

"The results of your psychological testing confirm your hostility and dependency on men. You have probably been dependent on every man in your life, starting with your father. The problem with being male-dependent is that a woman ties all her feelings of self-worth into what men think about her, what they do and say. You need to begin to become responsive to yourself and your own needs. You are a 'people-pleaser' like most alcoholics—and the people you try hardest to please are men."

For several moments I was silent, devastated by this appraisal that I knew deep-down to be true. "How do I get free?" I finally asked.

"For the next four weeks you will be on a 'male restriction' program. This means you will not have anything to do with men. You can write or call one male member of your family once a week, but you're to avoid conversations with men, even eye contact with men on the street. You need to learn to trust women and the feedback they have for you."

At first this program seemed peculiar and unfair. Four weeks without talking to a man except my father, Brent, or Brad once every week or so? Impossible.

But it wasn't. I discovered how automatically I sought to make eye contact with men—in restaurants, at meetings, anywhere— even with total strangers. Somehow the approval of these nameless outsiders mattered. I'd be buoyed by a flicker of interest, dejected by indifference. It was a searing discovery.

"The notion that men are absolutely vital to any value we may have," writes Nancy Friday in *My Mother/My Self,* "is so woven into feminine reality that most women think to reject it would be like trying to reject the law of gravity."

Friday recalls in her book that "it was the promise of men, that around each corner there was yet another man, more wonderful than the last, that sustained me. You see, I had men confused with life. . . . It was a religion of a god who gave and took away life. . . ."

Psychologist Sonya Friedman in her book *Men Are Just Desserts* points out one of the most deeply ingrained messages that daughters receive from their mothers: *A man is the measure of your worth.*

To break the cycle of male dependency, then, it was apparent that I needed to enhance my sense of self-worth completely apart from men. And, in fact, after the first few days of my male restriction program, it became a little easier. Each time I resisted looking at a man for approval represented a victory. I was greatly encouraged. My self-esteem was growing in little flutters, but growing. By the end of the four weeks, I sensed a new strength in this area.

Other revelations: Male dependence had strangled my development as a person, kept my maturing process on hold. I'd often given up decision-making and goal-setting to comply with what the "he" in my life dictated. I had not learned to make responsible choices.

It was disconcerting to realize how early I'd begun to depend on male approval of my behavior, my appearance, my plans. An occasional desire for this kind of approval is normal and good, of course, but needing it constantly had long since become an unhealthy way of life.

Robin Norwood explains in *Women Who Love Too Much* that "a woman who uses her relationships as a drug will have fully as much denial about that fact as any chemically addictive individual, and fully as much resistance and fear concerning letting go of her obsessive thinking and high emotionally charged way of interacting with men. But usually, if she is gently but firmly confronted, she will at some level recognize the power of her relationship addiction and know she is in the grip of a pattern over which she has lost control."

You can test yourself for "Male Dependency" with the quiz on page 238.

An important aspect of my halfway house program was to reach a point where I could go out into the world and not only acquire a job, but succeed in it. Before I was ready for this step, my counselor felt I needed special preparation.

"Sandy, it's time for you to attend the assertiveness class," Betsy told me one day. She explained that the recovering addict needs to learn how better to handle confrontational situations without waffling or being dishonest. These four everyday situations, for example:

1. A salesclerk won't refund your money.

2. You ordered a steak medium-rare and it comes to the table well-done.

3. Your car wasn't repaired the way you specified.

4. A door-to-door salesman persists in trying to sell you something you don't want.

In the assertiveness class we were taught to "hang in there" for our viewpoint. Here is a typical role play:

Clerk: "May I help you?"

Me: "Yes. I'd like a refund of $85.99 on this vacuum cleaner."

Clerk: "We don't give refunds."

Me: "I understood that if I brought in the receipt, you would refund my money. Here is my receipt. I'd like my money back."

Clerk: "I'm not supposed to give refunds. I'll get in trouble."

Me: "I'm sorry for you if that happens, but I still want my $85.99 refunded."

Clerk: "Why don't you take the vacuum cleaner home and try it out for another week? Get used to it."

Me: "I want my $85.99 or your name and the name of your supervisor."

Clerk: "I'm not supposed to do this, you know," as he takes the receipt and refunds the money.

In the above exchange I was instructed to state persistently what I wanted and avoid being sidetracked onto irrelevant issues. (The person playing the clerk was told to resist in every possible way.) My ace in the hole was what I had been told initially about the store's general policy regarding refunds.

Learning such basic life skills was essential before we recovering alcoholics were ready to enter the rough-and-tumble of the job market. Even with this training, the thought of having to interview for employment paralyzed me. My work as an artist at Disneyland and my public relations position with Pepsi Cola had been over twenty years ago. Who would want to hire a forty-four-year-old has-been? Was I employable?

For two days at the Office of the Civilian Employment Training Agency (CETA), five of us from Jane Dickman House underwent intensive schooling on how to conduct ourselves at a job interview. Then weeks passed and the only work that became available for me was through an office temporary service. Stuffing envelopes for mailings didn't pay much, and at the end of the day my fingers were covered with Band-Aids to cover the paper cuts. "I'll never get a decent job," I moaned. "How am I ever going to support myself?"

Then CETA phoned. "The Minnesota Museum of Art is looking for an assistant preparator of exhibitions. Call and set up an interview . . . and good luck!"

What do you wear for an interview with three museum directors? I had visions of three dour faces peering at me from behind a mahogany, skating-rink-sized conference table. What a shock to find three laid-back, obviously creative, no-nonsense professionals in tweeds and corduroys chatting merrily, drinking coffee.

The business administrator asked most of the questions. I liked her immediately. Her pale blue eyes danced in a thin, angular face. She'd be enjoyable to work with. "Do you have any carpentry skills?" she asked. "You'll need to be able to do a little bit of everything around here."

"My father taught me how to build and paint and wallpaper," I offered. "Even how to do simple plumbing and electrical work."

The director's eyes lit up. "I had pictured giving this job to a man," he said, "but if you think you could handle the physical demands, you might be the one for it. We have a number of others to interview today before we decide. Thanks for your time."

I was waiting for him to say, "Don't call us, we'll call you," but he didn't.

Back at the halfway house I lunged for the phone each time it rang. Hours later the administrator called, "We've reviewed all the applications and have narrowed it down to two. I need to ask you a crucial question: do you know how to drive a truck?"

My mind was racing. I really wanted that job. Could I drive a truck? Of course! But my conscience was saying, *You've driven only a pickup truck.* Clearing my throat, as if to convince myself first, I replied, "I can drive a truck just so long as it isn't an eighteen-wheeler."

"Great," she responded. "The job is yours."

I held the job for seven months until my counselor felt I was ready to go back home to Billings. It was a valuable experience, bolstering my sense of self-worth and rekindling my creativity. It felt so good to be productive again.

A sign of my walk toward wholeness was the interest I began taking in other women and their problems. A seed was growing inside me of love for people. The capacity to reach out had withered during twenty years of addiction, only to sprout anew that night in the Warm Springs Hospital when I comforted Karen.

One of the patients at the halfway house with whom I developed an almost mother-daughter relationship was a seventeen-year-old named Sophia. She was a pretty girl with brown hair and a face that didn't show her drug and alcohol abuse. Sophia had started drinking when she was in the third grade. In the sixth grade she was introduced to marijuana; two years later she began using hashish, speed, and LSD.

At fifteen Sophia moved out from her family and in with a boyfriend, got a cleaning job at a bar, and was soon drunk morning, noon, and night. She'd recently spent a month in treatment, then entered Jane Dickman House.

I was attracted to Sophia because she was close to the age of my daughter Lisa (then eighteen) and so needy for love and attention. Treatment had given her some handles on her disease, but her counselor and friends wondered if these would be broken when she returned to her old environment and faced both chemically active friends and a male-dependent relationship.

The issue came to a climax one March afternoon. Her boyfriend—I'll call him Nick—rolled into the parking lot on his motorcycle and bellowed for his "woman." Sophia hadn't seen Nick in six months.

Her roommate and I went outside to talk with him. Nick measured about six-two and looked at us with sullen, half-closed eyes. "Where's Sophia?" he demanded.

"She says she doesn't want to see you," her roommate told him.

"I want *her* to tell me that."

Reluctantly Sophia came outside and faced the past. Several of us formed a protective semicircle behind her while Sophia stared at Nick in silence. We could all feel the power he held over her. Bluntly he ordered her to come with him.

I knew well what was going on inside of Sophia. On the one side, a pull toward sex, drugs, alcohol; on the other, freedom from the cravings, the beginning of a new self-worth. The choice: Hop onto Nick's bike and return to her old life, or stay with us and continue being healed.

She turned and looked at us, the people who had befriended her. No one spoke, but something clicked. A decision. She turned to the biker: "No, I don't want to see you ever again." His eyes intensified, bore hard into hers to test her resolve. Then, with a shrug, he got onto his bike and roared away.

Each woman who goes through the program at Jane Dickman has a personal graduation ceremony. Mine was highlighted by a visit from Lisa, generous tributes from the staff, other patients, and friends I'd made in the area. First steps had been taken in leaving anger and male dependency behind. It was time, as Sonya Friedman writes in *Men Are Just Desserts,* to reassess my skills, my personality, my self-esteem.

"The more you are," she says, "the more you possess yourself without getting caught up with pleasing others and the more you can understand that no one's going to make you happy, or complete, but yourself. The more you *are,* the more you will realize that a man can detract from or enhance your happiness, but he can never be responsible for answering all your needs."

13

Deception and
Other Little Monsters

The key word in [self-cure] is self: taking charge of your own problem. Some psychologists call this self-mastery; others, self-efficacy; others, the belief in free will. It translates into three components necessary for change: an urge to quit, the belief that you can quit and the realization that you must quit—no one can do it for you.

—Stanton Peele, Ph.D.
"Out of the Habit Trap"
American Health

RECOVERY IS NOT ONLY A PROCESS; IT'S A PROCESS THAT TAKES TIME. A lot of time.

Treatment programs—whether they last a month or a year—are only a beginning. A turnaround. The compulsive person is given a temporary sanctuary, a direction to go, guidelines to follow. He's then released into the world, at which point the real battle begins. One chemical dependency specialist estimates that fifteen percent of recovery occurs in treatment, the other eighty-five percent in the outside world.

When I came out of nearly eight months of treatment at Jane Dickman I asked myself, "What have you learned?"

A great deal. I knew, for example, that one drink—just one—could start an avalanche inside me that would propel me down, down, down to destruction. This was not theory. When I emerged from twenty-eight days of treatment in Minneapolis that first time, back in 1977, I abstained for two months, then decided to have a single drink. What followed was disaster.

Later I had well-meaning church friends tell me I was now free of my bondage and that an occasional drink would not trigger a relapse. I consider that deadly advice.

Besides, even if it were true that I could take a drink without ill consequences, I wouldn't do it. I've come to love the way I feel alcohol-free. I like the clear head, the aliveness. One drink would bring on the dullness I remember too well. What I thought was stimulation was the very reverse. The seduction of alcohol is that you feel you are getting sharper, brighter, wittier, while the exact opposite is occurring. You are getting duller, more sluggish, merely silly. I want no part of that second-class existence now that I've lived first-class for years since that Valentine's Day 1980.

I'd also learned that *recovery means civil war.* Back home I would literally be going to war with myself and my old destructive habit patterns. After nine months of treatment the battleground was clear to me. It involved change—change across-the-board.

Fortunately, most treatment centers offer an "aftercare" plan. Mine covered the obvious things I'd already been working on:

Anger

Male dependency

Food issues

Shopping/spending

Perfectionistic behavior

To help me abstain from chemicals, I was to be involved with a continuing alcohol support group.

I was to talk about and express my feelings with someone daily.

I was to get regular exercise.

I was to watch my nutrition carefully.

As I picked up the routines of living, I discovered that the danger was not going to be so much from the big monsters that had nearly destroyed me, as from a lot of little ones. Reentry into Billings, Montana, where I had been so sick, was painful. There were old relationships to sort through and mend, new ones to contemplate. Most importantly, my grown children lived and worked there. My dearest wish was to reestablish warm, healthy relationships with them. They were so mature in some ways, self-reliant from years of fending for themselves. Yet also hurting and vulnerable, watching me with guarded enthusiasm. Is this really Mom? Is she going to be okay? In some ways we were almost strangers.

Sometimes at night as I lay sleepless in the small apartment I'd moved into, I tried to piece together the fragments of lost years with them. What had happened during their junior and senior high school years? Those were the years I was mostly out-of-it. I felt robbed of so many milestones in their lives. In my remorse I tried to think of ways to make up these losses to my children. It wasn't possible, of course. The damage done was real and could not be erased by guilty efforts at compensation. In fact, my counselor had warned me that if I focused too much on trying to undo the past, it would not only sabotage my recovery but confuse my children in unhealthy ways.

So each day I tried to deal with this little monster of *if-only*. If only I hadn't . . . whatever. The best method was to focus on today and be grateful for how far I had come. I tried to start each day in this frame of mind, dressing quickly before six A.M., bounding down the stairs of my small third-floor apartment, and walking a three-mile route I'd laid out around the city, before digging into my work of costume-and-doll designing for a Boston firm.

There was something therapeutic about being out in the crisp morning air—more so than the compulsive morning exercising at the Y that had been so unproductive. I'd read that walking was good for patients suffering from depression and now I could understand why. All body systems seem to tune up when you're walking. The senses expand to enfold everything about you.

As I passed the Deaconess Hospital on my route, I offered prayers for the patients on the psych ward where I had spent several "drying-out" periods back in the mid-1970s. Looking up at the fluorescent-lighted ceilings on the second floor, I recalled the countless hours I stared at those very light fixtures, and watched forlornly out the window at people bustling up and down the same streets I now walked in health and growing freedom.

Another of the little monsters I sought to overcome was the monster of *lying.* This was an especially difficult part of my recovery program—to change my deceitful nature into an honest one. The problem is that lying becomes a way of life for the addict. We start by lying to ourselves: "I couldn't have done that. I just *wouldn't* behave that way."

Later my behavior in blackouts had to be covered with lies because I couldn't remember what I'd said or where I'd been. I lived in a constant state of fear because I couldn't remember large blocks of time—what I'd done, how I'd gotten home. The blood spattered on our white Jeep, for example, that had caused me such apprehension. Many were the mornings I raced to the garage to see if my car was in its usual spot.

All of life thus becomes a lie. Even my sober times were colored with various shadings of the truth. I was wound about like a mummy with layers and layers of deception. My ears were deaf to the truth; my eyes saw only a miniscule slice of reality.

When I started working my recovery program, I knew I had to get honest with both myself and other people. Especially with myself. My conscience became newly activated. As soon as I told a lie, a searing stab of conviction would hit me.

Once, counting my change outside the grocery store, I realized that the checker had mistaken a ten-dollar bill I'd given her for a twenty. This came at a time when I was short of funds. But I went back into the store to return the money. It was a small act, but represented growth.

Cash-register honesty came more easily than more subtle challenges. At the beginning of my rehabilitation, I promised myself I wouldn't lie for one whole day. It was interesting to see how quickly little fibs and exaggerations tended to creep into my conversation. A friend asked me over the phone how I liked the book she had loaned me. "I'm getting a lot out of it" slipped off my tongue. A white lie, but still deceptive. The truthful reply should have been, "I'm looking forward to reading it this weekend."

I was interested much later to note a similar push toward honesty in an article by Dr. Sirgay Sanger in the newsletter of the National Council on Compulsive Gambling (Winter 1985). He identifies even accepting too much change in a store as a serious ethical problem that often leads to behavioral relapse.

"I have yet to see compulsive gamblers who have been lying and cheating not fall back into gambling," he observes. "What I usually recommend is a complete dedication to honesty and integrity in as many areas as possible."

My own daily effort at truthfulness showed me how inclined I was to deny unpleasantness, always to paint the rosy picture. The most staggering realization was how I minimized or lied about my feelings. As my time of sobriety lengthened, real feelings that I had medicated for years started emerging. Unwrapping those endless layers of cover-up was agony. Lies had been my armor, my protection. Now I stood shivering in naked vulnerability with no place to escape.

An especially nasty little monster was *profanity.* I had started swearing in high school because it seemed sophisticated, and I progressed to the point where bad language was an automatic knee-jerk reaction to things that went wrong—or even right. Once

I overheard a woman tell her husband in hushed tones what a foul mouth I had. I dismissed it as the utterance of a prude.

Now I felt uncomfortable saying, or even hearing, four-letter words. Yet they still slipped out—sometimes at the most inopportune times.

Though I've begun to make progress in this area, I don't kid myself. Lurking in my compulsivity is a little monster that has been exposed, rebuked, and reduced to a whimper. But it hasn't left the premises.

My behavior is often at war with my will. I want to be disciplined, but it's as though my desire world has metastasized, with each tiny fragment capable of spawning a cancerous growth of its own.

Another monster with which I've had to deal is *shopping*. Like so many hurting women, I used spending binges to fill the emptiness in my life. In 1976, for example, my work as a sales clerk in Billings' largest department store was a disastrous experience economically. Each day I bought at least one item, rationalizing I was saving money with my employee's discount. At month's end my store bill far exceeded my salary.

Somehow loading my arms with bundles and boxes relieved my sense of low self-worth, made me feel important, cared for. What I didn't realize was that this is addictive behavior as surely as drinking and drug-taking.

"It is well known," wrote Erich Fromm in his *Anatomy of Human Destructiveness*, "that . . . compulsive buying is one attempt to escape from a depressed mood . . . a symbolic act of filling the inner void and, thus, overcoming the depressed feeling for the moment."

After the well-publicized spending excesses of Imelda Marcos, it is interesting that Tammy Faye Bakker, in the height of the so-called "holy war" among television evangelists, confessed on ABC's *Nightline* to prodigious shopping and bargain-hunting because it "helps my nerves. It's cheaper than a psychiatrist."

During my recovery period I saw my own shopping binges for what they were— saw the shallowness of them, saw the disastrous outcome in domestic strife and economic setbacks.

Back in Billings I put myself on a budget. I'd always moaned that this was too hard, that I couldn't do figures. I found, of course, that anyone can do figures if she tries. But I still have to be careful when I'm tired or upset; at such moments shopping can become my fix.

Today when I pass stores advertising *Sale!* I ask myself, "Do I need this?" If I start to enter a store I ask, "Why am I going in here?" The temptation to spend always begins with the thought *I want this.* I'm gradually learning to counteract this thought with the question of need. If the desire won't stand cold, hard scrutiny, then I don't really want it at all.

In fact, all my problems, it seems, begin in my thought life: *I'll eat just this one cookie, I'll just browse at this sale and not buy anything. I'll take just one drink.* These thoughts and a myriad of others have to be brought under control.

Do's and Don't's for Compulsive Shoppers
Do's

1. Work out a systematic budget and stay with it. Be aware of where almost every penny goes.

2. List all your debts on a large wall calendar as a constant reminder.

3. Set a goal to get out of debt. The benefits, such as peace and delight, will be well worth it.

4. Stay with whatever plan you devise. You will often want to stop. Don't rationalize by saying, "I can skip a month; it's too much trouble to keep records."

5. Always pay bills before spending money on other things.

6. Use the income from a secondary source or from a working spouse basically for savings, investments, or paying off existing bills and loans. From *Money: How to Spend Less and Have More* by David J. Juroe

Don't's

1. When you see a sale sign, you don't always have to stop.

2. Remember that if you don't need something, it is not a bargain at any price, even if it is on sale.

3. Limit the cash you take with you on trips. If you have more, you may spend it.

4. Be careful about setting dates for entertainment or events where you know you will overspend, if you can't afford it.

5. Don't add new debts. This is very important. Why not call for a family gathering and make definite plans to cut spending?

6. Don't use credit for small items. Concentrate on paying cash for everything, even if you're in debt.

7. Don't throw away "junk." Much of it may be useful to someone else. So why not consider a sale at your house, like a yard or garage sale? Then use the money to pay off old debts.

Procrastination was another little monster that threatened the recovery process. "I'll do it tomorrow" was deeply ingrained. I'd rail at my daily schedule, want to stare out the window or chat on the phone. The *Do it now!* philosophy was helpful in this area. Slowly but surely I watched my life taking on healthy structure.

Each morning I made a list of the things that needed to be accomplished that day, trying to prioritize the three most important items and get them done before noon. I also included in my schedule times for recreation and rest. As one who had wasted so much time, rest was hard for me to take. I felt I needed to make every waking moment count until I realized my body couldn't physically meet those kinds of demands.

Whenever I attacked a compulsive pattern in my life, the little creepy crawler monsters would start to undermine my progress. *Food* and *shopping* continued to be booby traps, probably because I couldn't simply eliminate these areas of my life. Unlike alcohol or cigarettes, where the best—the only—answer for the compulsive woman is total abstinence, we all have to eat and we all have to go into stores. For the compulsive personality, moderation is the hardest achievement of all.

For a while I'd do fine on a reasonable regimen of eating. Then—most often in the late afternoon—I'd be attacked by what I called the "hungry horrors." Stricken, I'd dash to the refrigerator or out to a nearby convenience store for a pound bag of chocolate-covered peanuts, one of my choice binge foods. This would in turn trigger a desire for more sugar, more pastry, anything with white flour. I'd been warned at Dickman House that I was a "wheataholic." (*Why not,* I had thought. *I seem to have been every other kind of "aholic" there is.*)

The tendency to rush to the refrigerator when things go wrong can be compulsivity at its worst. Fortunately, I had friends now to help me face down the food monster. They steered me to a group of singles in Billings who met for meals and fellowship often during the week. This accomplished three things. It made me: (1) eat on schedule; (2) choose nutritious foods; (3) retain the companionship I needed to strengthen my self-discipline.

Several of us in the singles group who had similar eating problems benefited from a list of alternatives to food-binging. Here are some steps we learned to take.

When the Urge To Binge Is Overpowering:[11]

1. Call a group member or friend. Keep calling until you reach someone.

2. Write the binge down instead of eating.

3. Take a bath or shower.

4. Take a walk.

5. Do a non-food-related activity outside the kitchen. Stay out of the kitchen.

6. Go to an eating disorder support group meeting.

7. Do a relaxation exercise or meditation.

8. Distract yourself with a craft project, book, or TV program.

9. Read something inspirational or positive.

10. Run or jog.

11. Take a nap.

12. Engross yourself in something.

13. Go to a concert, play, etc.

14. Think the binge through—"what I'll get out of it."

15. Put the binge off five minutes at a time.

16. Write down the things you want out of life.

17. Write down the things you've missed because of binging.

The following guidelines to good eating habits can be helpful:

1. Eat slowly and chew well—especially when emotionally upset.

2. When eating, only eat. No other activities such as TV, radio, reading, or driving.

3. Eat sitting down at a table.

4. Clear the table immediately when through eating.

5. Know what you're going to do after a meal—have a plan.

6. Throw leftovers away. It's okay!

It was also helpful to remember that it takes twenty minutes for our stomachs to register a "full" feeling. I tried to stop eating *before*

I felt full. The best defense I found against the hungry horrors and other assaults was to begin each day with an admission of my helplessness and dependence on God.

My religious faith has played a growing role in my overcoming these and other "monsters." A verse from the New Testament book of Romans is interesting, in this regard: "I do not understand what I do. For what I want to do I do not do, but what I hate I do."[12] This internal warring describes the compulsive woman to a T, and I am as dependent as the writer of these words in finding success by turning to Jesus Christ, my Higher Power, when I am overwhelmed by the temptation to succumb to one of my former compulsions.

The same biblical writer talks in another place about bringing "every thought captive" to Christ.[13] Is this God's suggestion to those of us who are dealing with compulsivity?

Many women, of course, do not choose this way of dealing with it. I understand. Regardless of a person's religious orientation, it is imperative only that she practice some form of quieting herself, of centering down, of broadening her perspective on life.

"Develop your spirituality through daily practice," advises Robin Norwood in *Women Who Love Too Much.* "Whether or not you have a belief in God, and if you do, whether or not you're on speaking terms with Him, you can still practice this step. . . . Even if you are a 100-percent atheist, perhaps you get pleasure and solace from a quiet walk, or contemplating a sunset or some aspect of nature. Whatever takes you beyond yourself and into a broader perspective on things is what this step is all about."

Along the way to recovery I found it necessary to break off relationships with old drinking friends or those who had "enabled" me when I was ill. As I expected, some heaped scorn on me as "self-righteous" or "judgmental" or "a lousy friend." Later, when I'm stronger, perhaps I can seek them out to try and establish relationships on a new basis.

Other good advice that came to me along the way:

"Stay in the present! Yesterday is a canceled check. Tomorrow is a promissory note. Today is ready cash. Spend it wisely. Enjoy life where you are right now."

Whenever I forgot and started to dwell on the past, I was dragged down into a numbing state of depression. Actually, I thought of it as a "depressionetta," a mere niggle compared to the crashing bottoming-out of the past. What helped me was having a meditation time while I walked in the morning and a prayer time when I took my personal inventory before retiring for the night. As I struggled through a succession of difficult choices day by day, I was chasing the little monsters out of my life.

"It takes time, effort, and faith to mature out of an addictive disposition," declares Stanton Peele, one of the foremost authorities on addiction. ". . . Therapy or no, the ultimate responsibility is still our own" [*Love and Addiction*].

In taking responsibility for my own recovery, and in breaking the pattern of negative thinking I've engaged in for most of my life, I'm learning to get my feelings out on the table, look them over, and realize they can be changed. One procedure is through simple positive statements such as the affirmations:

Changing the Negative to Positive[14]

1. I [your name] like myself. I am a lovable person.

2. I have the right to say no to people without losing their love.

3. Other people have the right to say no to me without hurting me.

4. I am building a perfectly functioning body.

5. I affirm health, harmony, peace, and abundance.

6. I am giving my subconscious mind a new blueprint for my life.

7. I am calm, relaxed, serene, and confident.

8. Smoking no longer appeals to me.

9. I am developing a taste for non-fattening foods.

10. Every day I am becoming more aware of things for which I can be thankful.

11. I have now enough time, energy, wisdom, and money to accomplish all my desires.

12. I have an abundant supply of energy and draw upon it at will.

13. I have an excellent memory and it is getting better every day.

14. I am well-organized in every phase of my life, giving me time for leisure.

15. I am able to relax as deeply as I wish at any time.

16. It is safe for me to love and trust people and to accept the love and trust that is my birthright.

17. I see myself in my right job, performing it completely and easily.

Learning to Like Yourself

Learning to fulfill our needs must begin early in infancy, and continue all our lives. If we fail to learn we will suffer, and this suffering always drives us to try unrealistic means to fulfill our needs. A person who does not learn as a little child to give and receive love may spend the rest of his life unsuccessfully trying to love.

—William Glasser, M.D.
Reality Therapy

*F*OR YEARS I'VE ASKED MYSELF WHY SOME PEOPLE CARRY AROUND SUCH A low self-image when they're as richly endowed with gifts and talents as anyone else.

In my case I've identified some partial answers dating to childhood. An early episode of sexual abuse produced in me a sense of shame because I felt somehow it was my fault that it happened. The silent, unhappy home where emotions were not acknowledged soon made me ashamed of any strong feelings. When eventually my parents divorced I felt still more shame, believing that undoubtedly this was my fault, too.

The root of compulsive behavior, as we have already seen, is shame. To compensate for my own shame, I became an overachiever and people-pleaser. This way I didn't have to face my own pain, anger, fear, and guilt. My constant attempts to win approval led me into a pattern of obsession about my appearance and the neatness of my surroundings. If everything looked impeccable on the outside, no one would ever know that inside there was such a mess.

Because I couldn't love myself, I searched for others to love me, especially men, even though subconsciously I didn't trust them. I was desperate for the reassurance that I was lovable. When these relationships didn't work out, I sought my reassurance from alcohol and food. My search for some sense of worth and meaning led me into a cult that left me haunted with more self-hate and condemnation than before. Soon all my compulsive behaviors and dependencies became woven together in a spiderweb trap. I'd break through in one area only to be strangled in another.

In thinking back to when my suicidally low self-image began a turnaround, I've identified some early steps:

1. Karen singling me out in the hospital as her friend. Her need compelled me to give instead of take.

2. Making a list of simple things to do my first day at home from the hospital—and then getting them done.

3. Making a successful case before the staff for my discharge from the hospital.

4. Stopping smoking.

5. Stopping drinking.

These action-steps may not even have been as important as the corresponding changes that took place in my mind and spirit. These changes, harder to trace, began at that magical moment in the hospital when I remembered a Scripture verse learned as a child: "By his stripes we are healed. . . ." I knew then my mind was not damaged beyond recall. The changes that followed revolved around the fundamental—and astonishing—awareness that I didn't have to prove anything to God. To my amazement he loved me unconditionally.

Despite my insights into the origins of a poor self-image, and how this can change, developing a sense of self-worth was a painfully slow process. It's a strange thing to encounter the real you for the first time in middle age. Strange and frightening. What if I didn't like me, let alone love me?

I did love the new freedom—freedom not to have secrets any longer. Freedom to be open and honest. Being able to share in groups, learning to have my own opinions instead of parroting those around me, helped self-esteem grow. Gradually I began to feel more comfortable with myself. For years I had been running and hiding from myself, searching for answers everywhere but inside.

At the four-year mark of my sobriety I felt a sense of peace, of being on target. I had moved in March 1984 back to my home state of Vermont, taking a small house in Montpelier next to my mother's even smaller one. (My stepfather had died the previous spring.) I hadn't wanted to move so far from my children, but they were all in their twenties, out in the working world, driving their own cars, busy with their own friends. We had loving relationships though not intimate.

So I settled into my little house in Vermont, quick to commit to an alcohol support group. I also converted the raised hearth of my living room fireplace into a makeshift altar. I laid a white lace cloth on the bricks and placed on it a pair of my Aunt Ethel's candleholders with white candles. It was here I spent much time in quiet prayer and reflection.

Sometimes my mind went back to the people I'd hurt—used and abused—and to situations I had tried to forget. As I repented of my sins against husbands, children, parents, friends, I asked God to show me where amends were possible and where restoration had to lie with him alone; where trying to clear my own conscience publicly would only lay further burdens on those I had injured.

Still other times I thought of people I needed to forgive, of anyone against whom I had nursed a grievance, starting with Uncle

Ralph. I'd write the name on a scrap of paper, say a prayer releasing that person from my judgment, and ask God's blessing on his or her life. Then I'd touch the paper to the nearest candle and watch old resentments turn to ashes in the fireplace.

What lightness and exhilaration of spirit followed! One by one the closed doors of my life were being opened, as I did what in effect amounted to a personal housecleaning.

Along the way I discovered ten exercises that have helped me begin to find the creativity I had lost. Since people recovering from addictive behavior have to face up to their need for personal disciplines, I offer them to you:

Ten Disciplines to Restore Creativity

1. Go "lean" one day a week. This is not necessarily a fast. Some who use this discipline reduce their food intake to juices, clear soups, and a few crackers.

2. Write a letter complimenting someone—or make it a telephone call. Be specific: "I admire the stand you took for that minority housing project," etc.

3. Once a week do something you've very seldom (if ever) done before. Go to the ballet, walk through a museum, try out a new recipe, plant some flowers, attend a church service.

4. Be completely honest for one full day in everything you say or do. If you can't be honest about your boss's expansion plans or your friend's new outfit, for example, say nothing.

5. For one hour think or pray on one subject. Or divide the hour into two separate periods, each devoted to one concern.

6. Express a heartfelt regret or ask forgiveness for something negative you have said or done fairly recently to a friend, co-worker, relative, etc. Do this through a letter or telephone call.

7. Spend one day being totally concerned about other people. This can be accomplished through volunteer work, through visits to

a hospital, through helping a friend with housework, through intercessory prayer. Avoid talk about yourself, your ideas, your plans.

8. For a set period of time—at least a day, perhaps a week or longer—keep your conversations with close friends or acquaintances or chance encounters on his/her interests solely. Focus on drawing the other person out. Learn what he/she thinks, feels, is experiencing.

9. Plan your activity in minute detail for one whole day and then live with this plan unless emergency situations arise. Try to anticipate everything that will happen and schedule time for telephone calls, for rest, recreation, eating, etc. See how close you can stick to your plan.

10. Set aside one day for obedience. As best you can let God and/or others determine what you do (within reason, of course). Consider yourself a total servant for this day. See yourself as a willing tool or instrument to bring joy and encouragement to others.

In the course of my own recovery, I decided the single life must be what I was now called to. I'd attended a number of retreats and workshops on how to find fulfillment as a single. I discovered I could help hurting single women, especially the ones with alcohol or drug problems, and felt drawn toward this work.

Sometimes I thought about marrying again, but always dismissed the thought. Two failures there had battered my self-image as a desirable person. And yet . . . something deep within me yearned to be a genuine partner. Not the needy, confused Sandy of the past, compulsively seeking a man to solve my problems, but a real wife, able to give as well as take. Could I hope to believe I had become, in a real sense, a new woman, clean and pure as the freshly fallen snow on my Vermont rooftop? I thought about this often, that first winter back East.

As I began telling my story here and there, a publisher contacted me and suggested I write a book. My newly won self-confidence quailed before such an assignment. I borrowed a typewriter and spent long, frustrating hours in front of it. When it was obvious I didn't know what I was doing, the publisher suggested I attend the *Decision* Magazine Writer's School to be held in St. Paul, Minnesota, in August 1984.

Once out there, I pored over the week's schedule, wondering what courses to take. On Monday afternoon there was to be a workshop on Creative Ideas by a longtime *Guideposts* editor named Leonard LeSourd. Hmmmm. I needed creative ideas for sure.

Monday morning there was talk at breakfast about the LeSourd workshop and about the death of his wife Catherine. "He must be awfully lonely," one woman said. "They were so close." Everyone seemed to know this Catherine and said her name with reverence.

Catherine who? I wondered to myself, not wanting to show my ignorance. "I've read *Christy* seven times!" someone gushed. Finally someone said Catherine Marshall.

Beyond Our Selves! I'd carried her book around for weeks at the Warm Springs Hospital. I had flipped through the pages thinking, "This woman has it too put together for me." Several times I had stopped at the dedication page—*To Len*—wondering who he could be.

That afternoon I arrived at the auditorium early and found a seat directly in front of the speaker's podium. Soon a handsome gray-haired man wearing a blue-and-white striped seersucker jacket and light blue trousers stepped up to it. Why, as Len LeSourd began to speak, did my heart do a ridiculous flip-flop? I didn't know this man at all.

With so many people crowding around him after the talk, I felt shy about introducing myself. I walked out of the lecture hall regretting that I would never exchange even a word with him.

At dinner, however, Len chanced to sit at the same family-style table where I was. Somehow I found myself telling him about my struggle with alcoholism. To my amazement, tears formed in his slate-blue eyes. "I have a niece who is battling that problem," he said. "Would you be willing to write to her?"

He gave me her address and took mine. Noting that I lived in Vermont, he mentioned that he would be driving through New England later that month. "Maybe I'll give you a call."

Three weeks later in Vermont, my telephone rang. Len was in the area; could I make a room reservation for him somewhere nearby for Saturday night? He'd become such a workaholic since Catherine's death, he explained, that his family had needled him into taking this vacation trip through New England. "I'm supposed to stop regularly and smell the flowers."

I took that as a personal mission. I reserved a room at the Montpelier Tavern Inn, a historic spot where stagecoaches used to stop. Now for a surprise welcome.

Margaret, a creative friend of mine, and I borrowed the key to his room. We pinned a newsprint banner—*Welcome to Montpelier, Len!*—to the top of the drapes. On one of the twin beds, we placed a large black teddy bear, decked out in an antique lace collar and black hat trimmed with violets. Nestled next to the bear was a straw basket labeled *First-Aid Kit for the Weary Traveler.* In it was a box of Vermont maple candy, a clump of red grapes, imported crackers and cheese, and a bottle of aspirin.

On the small table by the picture window was a bouquet of black-eyed Susans. I smiled recalling how I'd picked them the day before in a drenching rain. Was my compulsive nature showing? Well, Len had admitted to a compulsive side, too.

Late in the afternoon the telephone rang again. Len was chuckling. "There seems to be a bear in my room. Does she have a name?"

"Yes. 'Golly.' "

"I see." A pause. "Is she a good roommate?"

"Oh, yes. She almost never snores."

After our first dinner date at the Trapp Family Lodge in nearby Stowe, Vermont, Len and I began to see a lot of one another. As the weeks passed and he kept discovering reasons to come to Vermont, we acknowledged that we were falling in love. At the same time, both of us were impressed by a principle we chose to govern our relationship: *The best comes out of self-denial.*

I'd known that with my mind all my life. Even as my compulsivity drove me to indulge every passion—whether for chocolate, clothes, booze, cigarettes—I'd known that a saner, healthier existence meant saying no to these things. What I'd never been able to do was make my *no* stick.

Now, because of the psychological, chemical, and spiritual healing taking place in me, I found a bracing kind of joy in self-denial. By forgoing a sexual relationship, Len and I became friends first, learned how to laugh together, got to know each other at a deeper level.

As weeks turned into months and the desire for marriage grew in us both, we set out to visit all members of our two families. The visit that showed me much about my recovery was when I joined Len for a weekend at his farm in Virginia, forty-five miles west of Washington. Living with him in her own wing at Evergreen Farm was his mother-in-law, Leonora Wood, whose exploits as an eighteen-year-old schoolteacher in the Great Smoky Mountains back in 1912 formed the basis for Catherine's novel *Christy.* Mother Wood, then 93, was the beloved and respected family matriarch. How would she receive me? And how would Len's friends and business associates respond to the new woman in his life?

After the Sunday morning service at Len's church, one woman with piercing gray eyes grilled me in a polite way, drawing out that I had been twice married and twice divorced and was presently unemployed because I was trying to write a book. Hardly a success story.

Nor was my time with Mother Wood encouraging. Though frail

and bent in body, Mrs. Wood was a towering personage with an active mind, mixed with the loneliness of a mother and grandmother who had said premature good-byes to a husband, two children, and three grandchildren. She was kind and courteous to me, but I sensed underneath a steely opposition. And why not? To her I must have seemed a brash outsider with designs on taking Catherine's place.

Wherever I went in the nineteen-room farmhouse, Catherine's presence preceded me. She smiled at me from dozens of photos about the home and office. Her serene gaze from a magnificent oil portrait in Evergreen's formal parlor met my own each time I came through the front door.

Only a few years earlier, I would have fallen into the trap of comparing myself with her. Shame-ridden people—compulsive people—do that. Finding no worth in themselves, they make other people the standard. Other people's achievements, other people's virtues.

I learned, happily, that I was far enough along in my recovery to realize that of course I could not take Catherine's place, or the place of anyone else. I was me. I'd spent the past few years getting to know me—and, wonder of wonders, I was beginning to like me.

Still, there came a bleak moment when I just wanted to flee. Clearly I didn't belong among these productive, successful people. In my despair I sought out Len and suggested I return early to Vermont. He looked at me, smiled, and shook his head.

"It's rough for you, Sandy, but you'll make it."

"But your family is so . . . put together. I'm still struggling, and I'm a failure as a wife and parent."

"You are not a failure. You're an overcomer. That's even better than being a success."

I knew for sure at that moment why I loved this man.

Other family get-togethers followed over the next few months—

with Len's three children and their two spouses, his stepson and family, my three children, and my parents.

The final green light for me came after the Mother's Day church service one May Sunday in Virginia. Len and I had taken Mother Wood there, packing her wheelchair into the trunk of the car. When I leaned down to release the brake before wheeling her out, she drew my face very close to her own and looked into my eyes with her incredibly intense blue ones. "I love you, Sandy," she said softly. "I'm so grateful you're going to be part of our family."

Len and I were married on June 22, 1985, at the Trapp Family Lodge, in Stowe, Vermont—ten months after our first date there the previous August. As we began to adjust to each other in marriage, we both took a hard look at compulsive behavior persisting into the present—mine and his. Len had been a workaholic and a sportsaholic. Forty years of meeting publication deadlines, often working past midnight and over the weekend, had produced an imbalance in his life. Often his change of pace came through a more-than-casual involvement in televised sports, especially pro football.

Len's emotional involvement with the Dallas Cowboys was a revelation. "To root for a team you need to read up on the players, coaches, get all the local color," he told me by way of explaining the pile of sports magazines by his chair.

"But why does losing a game take on more importance than a nuclear accident or a disastrous earthquake?" I asked.

Len looked reflective. "I'm powerless over my sports addiction and my life has become unmanageable," he said with a grin. Then, more seriously, he confessed to disturbance over the intensity, even destructiveness, of fans absorbed with a team, the ridiculous salaries of the players which often lead to drug use, the obsession with winning.

He admitted that involvement in a late-night game on television often rendered him sleepless for hours afterwards, wiping him out for most of the next day. Sunday afternoon games often assumed such importance, he further revealed, that he would duck social engagements, even family responsibilities, to watch his team play.

"Next Sunday I won't watch the game," he declared suddenly. "We'll go for a drive, smell the autumn leaves."

Next Sunday afternoon we did go out for a couple of hours. Upon our return he fidgeted miserably about the living room, then switched on the TV. Soon he was glued to the action. I watched him with bemused understanding.

For I'm still battling certain compulsions in my life. Shopping, for one. Sometimes I still come out of stores with more items than I planned to buy, and rail at myself later.

Then there was the time I made a special greeting card to celebrate the birth of one of Len's grandchildren. It started out as a simple card. Four hours later it had grown into a huge eight-color poster announcing *The First Annual Mary Catherine Lader Golf Classic*. The following day, playing golf with friends, Len and I displayed the poster on the back of our golf cart and sent photos of the "event" to Len's daughter and son-in-law.

It was this spontaneous "golf classic," silly but fun, that helped me understand something about compulsive behavior.

It's not all bad!

Along with certain native gifts and abilities, we often have an inner drive that helps us channel gifts into a successful career. We need the tenacity, the determination, the focused energy to achieve worthwhile things. Len's compulsion for work made him a topflight editor; my compulsion for quality—whether in dress design or floral displays—is also an exercise of my gift. The all-out effort poured into a project can make that project shine.

This was an important discovery for me. I'm not to crush my zealous nature, or scorn it. It's a part of me, a kind of inner dynamo given me for a purpose. Only for years I misused it. I let this driving quality inside, the "I-want-what-I-want-when-I-want-it" part of my nature, take over my life.

Now I'm striving to bring this compulsive part of me, like the rest of my being, under control. There are times when I try to take charge again, which we're all free to do. But I'm learning to catch myself.

In my early mornings, for example. As soon as we got married, Len and I began praying first thing in the day that God would take the inner drive we both have and guide it. This seems to be happening.

I also find continuous healing as I shift my attention away from myself to other people, focusing on the words *serve, give, teach, share.* As parents and grandparents, this involves Len and me with more than forty people in our family alone. But it doesn't stop there.

Len and I have begun conducting team workshops on the subject of compulsive behavior. Researching the subject has taken us to treatment centers around the country. What troubles me is that medical and religious programs do not work more closely together, since I received such solid help from both disciplines. The main differences stem from definition. The scientific world regards compulsive behavior as a disease—chemical or psychological or both. Christians consider it a sin.

It was a lift to find one treatment center that combines both approaches.

When we drove into the Dunklin Memorial Camp thirty miles west of Stuart, Florida, the spacious grounds were alive with activity: men on tractors, or wielding shovels, or hoisting furniture into the back of a mud-spattered pickup truck. This alcohol and drug treatment center was clearly a busy place.

We parked and entered a low stucco office building to receive a warm welcome from Mickey Evans, who over a twenty-three-year period has built a sizable complex out of eight hundred acres of Florida swamp. He eased his powerful frame into a desk swivel chair and got quickly to the facts:

"This is a center for male alcoholics and drug addicts," he began. "We can house about thirty. Most of the men are poly-addicted; we don't get 'simple' alcoholics today except a few older men. We don't detox here. That's done down at the center in Fort Pierce. The men come to us sober. They're here to work and learn. I tell each man, 'There's a waiting list to get into this place. If you want to stay here, you must earn the right. If you don't, I'll give your bed to someone who'll make better use of it.' "

Mickey went on to describe excruciating difficulties with cocaine-users, calling this drug "deadly beyond our understanding; it can stay in the system for up to ten months."

Then came words that elated me: "Some Christian programs treat addiction as a sin, which it obviously is. Sin simply means 'off-the-mark'—and these men's lives are certainly that. But some of these places go further and take the stand that alcoholism and drug addiction are *not* physical diseases. They shun all medical helps, including the Twelve-Step program. After twenty-three years, I've concluded that chemical dependence is both sin and sickness. We treat addictions as a disease and use the Twelve-Step program that stresses commitment to a Higher Power. Here the Higher Power is Jesus Christ.

"We insist each man have a quiet time first thing in the morning," Mickey continued. "He also must make a daily moral inventory of the past twenty-four hours. This helps him get in touch with the attitudes that are motivating him. Addicts have to change their attitudes before they can change their behavior. All the men keep a personal journal to record their insights into themselves. Also, some of them never knew prayer is a two-way street. I feel the quiet time—learning to listen as well as to speak—is the key to the whole program."

The work program is also crucial to the addict's recovery, Mickey explained. This includes kitchen duty, laundry, painting, ranch work, gardening, caring for the horses. Residents grow most of their food and raise their own beef.

Weekends are devoted to family programs, when wives and children come out to participate in various activities. Even spouses are asked to do a daily moral inventory. Mickey considers addiction a family disease: "Sometimes the wife and children are sicker than the addict himself."

The Dunklin Camp has seen some remarkable improvements in families on these weekends. "Often it's the first time they've been able to sit down and be honest with each other," says Mickey. "Also, the first time the patient has been thinking clearly enough to hear what his family has to say to him. We won't take a man unless his family will agree to be part of every weekend program."

At first addicts were taken in without charge. But as time passed Mickey became aware of the human tendency to take lightly what we get for nothing. Though the program is still financed largely by contributions, the fee is now set at a thousand dollars for each three months of treatment. Each family pays fifteen dollars for the weekend program.

If a man is too poor to pay, but does have a television set, a gun, or some garden tools, Mickey will accept these as payment. He is convinced that unless a man has some kind of material investment in his treatment, he tends to drift through it. For those who stay in treatment for one year, there is a ninety percent recovery rate.

When I asked Mickey about a comparable program for women, he said that one Dunklin graduate and his wife had recently started a program in the Orlando area, based on Dunklin procedures.

People helping people. That's the message I receive as I look back on all I've learned over the past ten years. Karen; my Filipino doctor at Warm Springs; my friend Lois Ann; Dirk, who intervened when I was flying without chemicals; my counselor Gwen. . . . The list goes on and on.

* * *

July 9, 1986, was an extraordinary day, as well as a traumatic one. Len and I had traveled to Billings, Montana, to visit my children and meet with certain groups. But I was apprehensive about a speech I was to give before two hundred women at the Warbonnet Inn.

As our hostess for the week drove me to the meeting, I looked at my old hometown with new eyes. So many familiar landmarks, most filled with painful memories. The Warbonnet Inn itself: twelve years before I'd come to this same hotel ballroom for that first Serenity Society conference. How dazed and confused and frightened I'd been back then! And how much worse after my involvement with that cult. Now I felt alive, filled with enthusiasm.

As the audience started arriving my excitement—and nervousness—mounted. Many of the women had been dear friends during the twenty-one years I had lived in Billings.

Kathy, my former neighbor, who had led me to the seminar and church where I received my healing.

And Hilda, the woman who had been more of a mother to my children as our housecleaner for twenty years than I had.

And the grocery store clerk, Shelly, who had helped me with my grocery list when I could barely function—who had loved me when I couldn't love myself.

I was delighted to greet my former mother-in-law who visited me faithfully when I was in the state mental institution and encouraged me during my dark years.

Best of all, my daughter, Lisa, who had taken the afternoon off from her work at a video store.

Never before had there been assembled in one room so many people I loved, so many who had touched my life: the women from the Thursday prayer group, some of my tennis and bridge club friends; friends from the singles group; even former babysitters.

After the introduction I moved up to the podium before these people, opened my mouth to speak . . . and instead broke down and wept. When I regained my composure, I told the story of my compulsive behavior, addictions, hospitalization and recovery, having a strange sense of being at one point or another *every woman* in the room.

Looking back on my life, I was overwhelmed with gratitude for the patience, love, and support of so many people: family members who always believed in me somehow during the darkest of times; close friends who never quit praying that a miracle would occur in my life; and a loving and forgiving God who brought me back from the pit of hopelessness. Now I could say with total conviction that there are no hopeless situations. A helping hand awaits anyone, everyone who reaches out for it.

For I knew only too well the frustration, the pain, the sense of failure, the depression, the desire to self-destruct that compulsive women feel at one time or another. I had been through it all and discovered there are no hopeless cases. There is a way through the darkness into the light. We compulsive women can be freed from our bondage.

The way is long but it's possible. It begins with a frank acknowledgment of the areas of our addiction, all of them—a surrender to the reality of the problem. Critical are the steps of self-forgiveness and forgiving others, going back as far as we can remember. Face any long-buried emotion; walk through it, not around it. A "feelings journal," like my anger diary, may be helpful in this. A support group is invaluable. Developing a relationship with a Higher Power is crucial.

Then come the building-up steps. Set a succession of reachable goals. Maybe the admonition *Do it now* will be as helpful to you as it is to me. Every small victory raises our self-esteem, lets us know we can succeed, that we can do something even better. At last we will be ready to move beyond focusing primarily on ourselves and reach out toward those around us.

What a great feeling it is to know we have stopped being takers—that at last we have something to give!

Notes

1. Martha Janssen, *Silent Scream* (Philadelphia: Fortress Press, 1983), 13, 83.

2. From a lecture by Terry Kellogg at the Compulsivity Clinic.

3. Isaiah 53:5.

4. From a pamphlet by Children of Alcoholism Foundation, Inc., 200 Park Avenue, New York, NY 10166.

5. Ibid.

6. Janet G. Woititz, *Adult Children of Alcoholics* (Deerfield Beach, Fla.: Health Communications, Inc., 1983).

7. John M. Leighty, "Smoking: How to Wrap It Up," *Washington Post,* 19 November 1986.

8. Margaret Hamburg, M.D., "The Nature of Craving," *Vogue,* August 1986.

9. Anderson A. Spickard, M.D. and Barbara R. Thompson, *Dying for a Drink* (Waco: Word Books, 1985).

10. Some materials in this chapter adapted from *Broken Promises, Mended Dreams* by Richard Meryman (Little, Brown & Co.). The anonymous woman in this book was a composite of several women, including Sandra Simpson LeSourd.

11. From materials distributed by Rogers Memorial Hospital, Oconomowoc, Wisconsin.

12. Romans 7:15.

13. 2 Corinthians 10:5.

14. Affirmations by Ann Larson from Compulsivity Clinic materials.